THE SS NORTH AMERICAN

Running Aground, A Rescue and Other Tales

By Gerry Bay

Published by Gerry Bay
at Amazon.com

Cover Picture Courtesy of Tom Drake, W4IWH

ISBN: 978-0-9961898-4-2

Gerald Bay, 416 Tepi Drive, Southbury, CT 06488

DEDICATION

To all the men and women who served aboard the SS North American and her sister ship, the SS South American.

Table of Contents

ACKNOWLEDGMENTS

My thanks for the following people for making this book possible by their suggestions and by letting me use pictures from their collections:

Thomas Drake, W4IWH, has collected an enormous amount of information about the Georgian Bay Line and the *North* and *South Americans.* His help with pictures, brochures and other memorabilia was invaluable. His pictures are identified by his amateur radio call letters, W4IWH

Mark Peter Sprang, Historical Collections of the Great Lakes, Bowling Green State University was a great help with obtaining pictures and historical information about Captain Picard. His picture credits are labeled BGSU.

Tom McKee maintains a website for the Inland Marine Radio History Archive: http://www.imradioha.org, which is full of great information. His pictures are identified by his amateur radio call letters, K4ZAD

Eric Takakjian, co-author of "Dangerous Shallows", a great book about diving the ghost ships sunk off of Cape Cod. He loved the *North* and was obsessed with finding her.

Audra Washay who took a rough manuscript and converted it into something readable!

Note: Unattributed photos and documents are from the author's personal collection.

INTRODUCTION

She was bigger than I expected, as I saw her for the first time...gleaming white, her sides speckled with portholes, her prow turned up like a proud mother. An amazing summer of adventure lay ahead including running up on a sandbar in the St. Lawrence River, rescuing a small pleasure craft in a Lake Erie gale and spotting a "flying saucer". I also would discover new talents as I joined the song and dance production that provided entertainment for the passengers and this led to striking up a beautiful summer romance with the show's lead singer.

The *S. S. North American* lay tied to a wharf on the Detroit waterfront. As I signed the paperwork to join the ship as one of its Radio Operators, I felt a tremendous sense of history because she was among the last of the Great Lakes passenger steamships; I also felt some apprehension since the ship's communications would be my responsibility during my watch. But, in 1960, as a college student approaching his junior year, I was just excited to get on board.

Steamship passenger travel began around 1817 when the *Frontenac* and the *Ontario* commenced operations. Additional ships were launched when the Erie Canal opened in 1825 allowing people from the east coast and New England to travel to the major cities on the Great Lakes. In the 1850s, railroad companies established steamship lines to move passengers and freight from the East Coast to the railroads heading out West. Most of these ships combined freight hauling capabilities with passenger accommodations.

The passenger ship industry on the Great Lakes exploded in the late 1800's before cars and planes opened up new travel options. If you lived in the Midwest, taking a cruise on the Great Lakes was "The Thing" to do, second only to rail travel. Many North Woods resorts, including The Grand Hotel on Mackinac Island, became popular destinations because they were reachable by steamship. Fares were in the $5-7 per day range and luminaries, including Ernest Hemmingway, often took cruises on the Great Lakes to enjoy the North Woods.

SS NORTH AMERICAN

The death knell for the Great Lakes passenger steamship business was the introduction of the jet engine and the construction of the interstate highway system in the late 1950s. People could now easily travel in their cars anywhere in the U.S. or take a plane to Florida or the Caribbean where they could cruise on ships inexpensively because of cheap foreign labor. The last pure passenger ships operating, the *North American* and her sister ship, the *South American,* ceased operations in 1964 and 1967, respectively.

The Chicago, Duluth and Georgian Bay Transit Company, popularly known as the Georgian Bay Line, owned the two *Americans* and a third ship, the *Alabama.* Robert Davis formed the company in 1913 with 35 investors who capitalized the company with $250,000. The objective of the company was to build and operate pure passenger ships on the Great Lakes. The first ship built was the *North American*, launched in 1913, which was highly profitable. Based on this, the *South American* was commissioned in 1914.

Built by the Great Lakes Engineering Works at Ecorse, Michigan, the *North American* was 280 feet long, had a 47-foot beam and drew 17-1/2 feet. Her engine was a 2200 horsepower, quadruple expansion steam engine that was converted from coal to oil in 1923. Her hull was high-grade steel and her topsides were wood. Her insides were opulent. Erik Takakjian and Randall Peffer in *Dangerous Shallows* describe her thus:

"The cruise ship's slim white hull, tall topsides, forward wheelhouse and twin stacks give the *North American* the look of an immense yacht from the roaring twenties. The ship has a yacht-like interior as well, complete with a ballroom, multiple dining rooms and a ladies card room. There are vaulted ceilings in the saloons. Silver oak raised paneling adds opulence to the bars and other public rooms. Corinthian columns support the dining rooms' ceilings. Clerestories bring in natural sunlight and moonlight. Cherry trim highlights the staterooms. Passengers flock to a verandah cafe and "Egyptian lounge" to see and be seen after their daily rounds of the promenade deck."

The *North American* followed a typical route from Chicago to Mackinac Island and then on to Detroit, Cleveland and Buffalo. The St. Lawrence Seaway had just opened in 1959 and this gave the ship the opportunity to take several trips up to Montreal. This was a major draw for the passengers since going through the Seaway locks was fascinating entertainment.

Sometimes the ship stopped in smaller towns like Charlevoix, Michigan. The whole town would turn out to greet the ship, including the local high school band, and the townspeople wore festive holiday outfits. The arrival of the *North American* was a big deal for these towns and the stores placed signs in their windows saying, "Welcome North American". When the ship left, the band played and the passengers threw streamers to give the ship a big sendoff.

The *North* and *South Americans* had almost a cult-like following. People fell in love with the ships and enjoyed the closeness with the college-age crew. The crew was like family rather than impersonal and invisible servers like on some of the ocean-going passenger ships. Passengers frequently celebrated birthdays and anniversaries on board and many were return customers, having sailed aboard for multiple previous years.

In command of the ship was Captain Russell A. Picard, a 20-year veteran of the Georgian Bay Line. Captain Picard joined the company in 1940 as the Third Mate aboard the *North American.* He also served as Second or Third Mate aboard the *South American* and the *Alabama.* Finally, after this long apprenticeship, he took command of the *North American* in 1957 and served until 1961.

I was a 20-year-old college student studying electrical engineering at Purdue University. I was skilled in radio communications, including Morse code and was fortunate to have landed a summer job as a Radio Operator aboard the *North American.* During my watch, I would manage the ship's communications including passenger ship-to-shore and public address announcements...quite a responsibility for a young man. And it did not escape my attention that I would be serving with about 100 college age women whom, I hoped, would look kindly on me in my sharp blue officer's uniform with gold striping and insignia.

The *North* was a fine and proud ship. Each summer, the passengers and crew experienced many adventures...each a story unto itself. The summer of 1960 had more than its share. The chapters that follow recount these tales. I hope that, by telling these stories, you will get a feeling for what it was like to work on a ship like this and to experience one of the last passages on one of the last of the great, passenger cruise ships on the Great Lakes...and to experience, through my eyes, a young man having the time of his life.

Figure 1: Transiting the Chicago Locks--W4IWH

Figure 2: Underway--BGSU

Figure 3: In the Chicago Locks--BGSU

Figure 4: Stern View Showing Poop Deck, Promenade Deck and Fantail--BGSU

Figure 5: Aerial View Showing Radio Shack Behind Stacks--BGSU

GRAND SALOON AND GALLERY. S. S. NORTH AMERICAN AND SOUTH AMERICAN.

Figure 6: Grand Ballroom and Cabins--W4IWH

A view of the Ladies' Lounge reveals the excellent appointments that are the last word in marine elegance on either the S S. North American or S.S. South American.

Figure 7: Ladies' Lounge-BGSU

Figure 8: Observation Deck--W4IWH

CHAPTER ONE

ABANDON SHIP!

The *North American* accommodated approximately 450 passengers who were serviced by about 160 crewmembers. She carried ten lifeboats, five to a side. I'm glad we never used them in a real emergency because it sure would have been crowded!

The fire extinguishing system consisted of an extensive network of pipes and pumps. Wooden ships and ships with wooden super structures were a fire hazard and many lives were lost in ship fires. For example, in 1949, the *Noronic* burned at the wharf in Toronto with the loss of 119 lives. Indeed, the official end of the *Americans* came in 1966 when congress ordered them to the docks citing fire safety concerns.

On board the *North*, "fire and lifeboat" drills were held frequently. An alarm was sounded and the crewmembers went to their assigned stations. The first exercise involved turning on the fire hoses to demonstrate that they were working okay. Then we went to the lifeboats. Sometimes the boats would be lowered and we would row around the harbor. This was a big effort, not only because of the rowing but because the boats had to be cranked up again by hand...hard work. (I was lucky because I was assigned to Lifeboat #1, and we had a modified electric drill that we could plug into the lifeboat winch instead of the hand crank).

The radio shack on top of the ship became my position for the fire drill. This position was very advantageous since I could stay dry while the water would frequently be blown onboard by the wind, soaking those below me. The mate would walk the decks to make sure everything was working properly. A crusty old seaman, he would curse me if I didn't have exactly the right angle on the hose to keep the water away from him. And, if the truth be known, my aim was a little off every now and then, and I had to blame his shower on a "wind gust"!

One day, in Buffalo, New York, we were at the docks, tied up to our port side. On our starboard side was an oiler refueling us. The oiler was basically a barge with a low flat deck covered with pipes to handle the fuel oil. There were no passengers on board so we were all just relaxing when Captain Picard announced that we were going to have a fire and lifeboat drill. This startled me since there was no place to point the hose and we certainly weren't going to lower the lifeboats...or were we?

The Captain ordered the fire hoses to be deployed. Usually, this meant we would also turn the water on to demonstrate that the pumps were working. As I looked over the side, I saw the men on the oiler looking up with concerned looks on their faces. A hose below me turned on and there was much swearing and shouting from the crew on the oiler. I felt that I should demur to avoid adding to the confusion.

Next, we went to our lifeboat stations. When we assembled, we discussed whether or not we should lower the boat. It was tempting to lower our lifeboat right onto the deck of the oiler. What fun! The Captain, who had been in the wheelhouse and couldn't see or hear what was going on, finally walked out on the wings to observe. We were completing our preparations for lowering our boat when the Captain grasped the situation and commanded us to stop. The men on the oiler below were already running for cover and were thankful to see us stop. As for me, I was disappointed that we didn't fully "abandon ship"...it would have been a whole lot of fun!

Figure 9: Lifeboat aboard South American (Sister ship)--W4IWH

CHAPTER TWO

RADIO COMMUNICATIONS

The "radio shack" was located on top of the ship right behind the smokestacks. The room was full of fascinating radio equipment with big dials and meters. A sign above the desk said, "WTBA", our radio call letters, and the room had a slight electrical equipment smell. A "bug" for sending Morse code and a microphone for radiotelephone communications resided on the desk. When I entered the shack for the first time, I instantly felt at home.

A rack of equipment six feet high and18 inches wide housing the main transmitter stood against the back wall. Today, these electronics would fit in a breadbox. The operating position was a folding chair in front of a simple built-in desk surrounded by shelves of equipment. Sitting right in front was a radio operator's, "piece of gold"...a Collins KWM-2, which, in ham circles, was known as the best transceiver around. It operated on a new mode of communications called Single Sideband or SSB. All of the regular voice communications on the Great Lakes at the time used the AM mode like a car radio. However, we “hams” knew that SSB was the wave of the future. The FCC authorized a special license to the ship to use SSB to communicate with our sister ship, the *South American,* and with a ship to shore station. In return, the FCC received the results of our experiments.

The Chief Radio Operator occupied the aft cabin on the starboard side. The cabin on the port side aft contained two bunk beds for the Second Radio Officer and me. I was the Third Radio Officer and junior to the other two, which meant I got the worst watch, 12-4 AM and PM. I had the top bunk of the bunk bed and my head was near the ceiling. I conked my head many times over the summer when I was suddenly awakened by the ship's "whistle", and a foggy day meant no sleep as the ship's whistle became a foghorn.

SS NORTH AMERICAN

Phil Shuman, my cousin, was the Chief Radio Operator. Two years older than me, Phil was returning for his third season aboard the *North American*. The previous fall, Phil regaled me with stories about his summer fun and adventures aboard the ship. I vowed then to obtain my commercial radio licenses and to join him the next summer. Phil encouraged me and smoothed the way for me to join the ship.

Phil was the engineer's engineer. A recent electrical engineering graduate of Northwestern University, there was nothing he couldn't fix; he was a magician with electronics. We used to joke that, if something wasn't working, Phil would just wave his hand over it and it would spring to life!

When I received my offer letter, I was surprised to see that I was hired as the Second Radio Officer aboard the *SS South American* because I assumed I would be on the *North* with my cousin. However, I subsequently received another letter stating that the *North American* needed a Third Radio Officer and the company asked if I was interested. Because the *North* put into Chicago...my hometown...and the *South* didn't, I gladly accepted even though it was a "demotion". Plus, I got to sail with my cousin. I earned a salary of $310 per month.

No personal computers, cell phones or satellite GPS existed in 1960. While the captain or mate could communicate over short distances with an FM radio in the pilothouse, radio operators handled weather reports, passenger ship-to-shore and offshore emergency communications, sometimes by using Morse code. They also handled all public address announcements. Thus, safety and comfort on the ship depended upon the radio operators.

Radio communications aboard Great Lakes ships began around 1910 using "spark gap" transmitters and Morse code and the Coast Guard required radio operators aboard ships. By the mid-1940s, radiotelephone service began to be implemented so that voices could be transmitted using AM radio signals. These radios were easier to use and the Coast Guard relaxed its rules in 1954 by no longer requiring radio operators aboard ships.

The Georgian Bay Line, however, continued to hire radio operators for the reasons spelled out in my offer letter:

"We of the Georgian Bay Line feel that we have a definite moral obligation to our passengers which we would not be fulfilling if we adhered strictly to the minimum standards of the new regulations. We are thinking not only of the added safety benefits which can be gained through having trained operators aboard but also of the satisfaction which our passengers receive in the knowledge that they can contact friends or be contacted at any hour of the day or night in the case of a personal emergency.

Secondly, in spite of the great strides made in radiotelephone communications we have learned through frequently repeated experiences that it is not yet as reliable as radiotelegraph communications and since we do have the telegraph equipment aboard our ships, we want to be able to use it when necessity arises.

Thirdly, it is our intention to carry trained men who are able and will do everything possible to keep the equipment in proper operating condition throughout the voyage. Except in the case of a major breakdown, we feel that our operators should be able to make necessary repairs immediately without waiting until the ship arrives at its home port."

It was not easy to become a licensed radio operator since it required both a radiotelephone and radiotelegraphy license from the Federal Communications Commission. The FCC required an applicant for a license to send and receive Morse code at 25 words per minute (about two letters a second) and to pass a comprehensive written exam on radio theory, rules and regulations. One of the proudest days of my life was when I passed the exam for my commercial licenses and qualified for service on the *North*.

It helped that both Phil and I were ham radio operators and had already passed extensive tests, including Morse code, to qualify for our ham licenses. In the days before computers, the local neighborhood "geeks" were hams. We would build our equipment by tearing apart old TV sets for parts or by modifying old military service gear. Thus, the innards of communications equipment were familiar to us and we could repair things.

As I settled my gear into the cabin for the first time, I met Henry Waite who would be the Second Radio Operator for a couple of weeks before Ben arrived for the summer. I also went forward and met the Third Mate, John Flynn, who would also be onboard temporarily before Mark Cross arrived for the summer. Later, when I met Mark, I found him to be a crusty mariner who swore constantly. At first, I didn't think he was very happy to have to rely on a young man for his communications but, as time went by, we developed a fine mutual respect for one another.

I also met Captain Russell A. Picard who seemed to be ready for social security. I remember wondering if he was still capable of handling a big ship like the *North*. As we shall see in the ensuing chapters, my take was prescient.

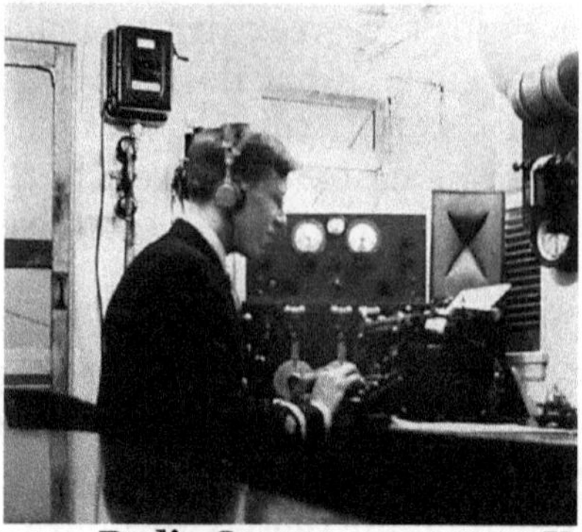

Figure 10: Radio Operator ca 1940--K4ZAD

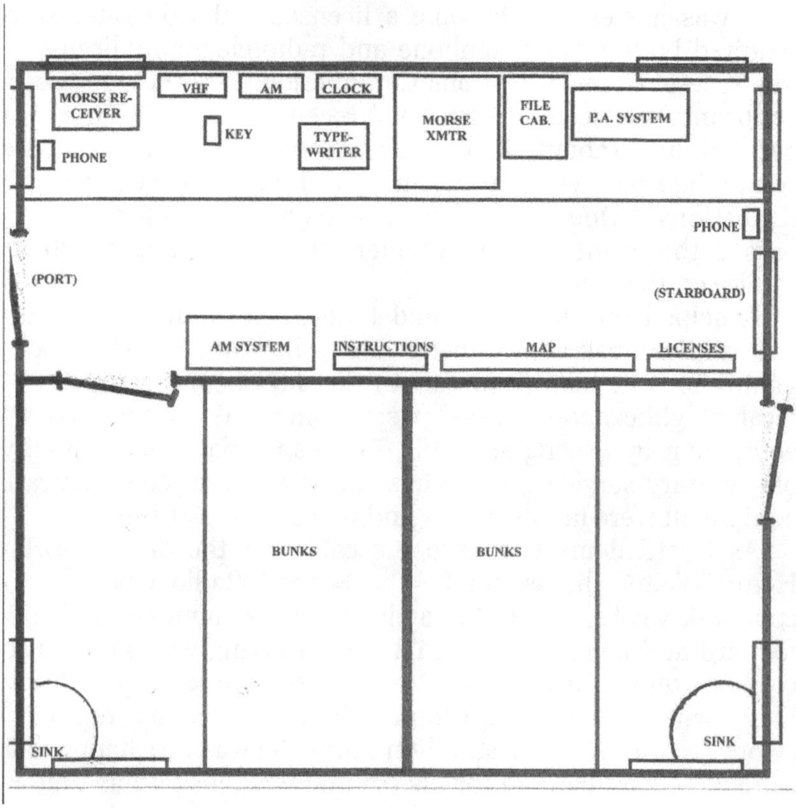

Figure 11: Layout of Radio Room--W4IWH

Figure 12: Inside of AM Transmitter-W4IWH

CHAPTER THREE

THE "CRUDE SHOW"

Today's modern cruise ships have world-class theaters onboard with orchestras, stage lighting and well-known entertainers. But in 1960, on a Great Lakes' steamship, the stages were small and rudimentary. Members of the crew, who performed song and dance numbers accompanied by a 4-piece band, provided the entertainment. Commonly known as "The Crew Show", Phil and Ben referred to it as "The Crude Show" and refused to participate thus showing their better judgment.

A professional music director/choreographer was onboard to put the show together and direct the volunteer crewmembers. These were simpler times and the passengers loved the intimacy of having one of their waitresses or busboys perform in the show. Fortunately, some crewmembers were studying music in school and had "opera" voices. They tended to carry the show and make up for the sometimes-awkward performances of the other volunteers.

During my first few days onboard, I met Joyce Jamison, the lead female singer in the Crew Show. Joyce did all the female solos and also the duets with a guy named Wayne. Their voices were outstanding. The rest of the volunteer crewmembers did song and dance numbers many of which were designed to be humorous so that the passengers didn't focus too much on the quality of the singing.

Joyce was an attractive blond and we hit it off immediately. She invited me to join the Crew Show. While Phil and Ben's "Crude Show" moniker signaled caution, the thought of hanging around Joyce overcame my fears and so I signed up. It wasn't long before we began a relationship that lasted through the summer and beyond.

THE "'CRUDE SHOW"

We began rehearsing, which was somewhat difficult because members of the cast frequently worked different hours. Initially, I joined a group choral number singing a Thanksgiving number, "Let All Things Now Living", which closed the show. I remember little about this number, which is probably a reflection on how well it went.

It soon became clear that anything the crewmembers lacked in musical ability was more than made up for with enthusiasm, although this exuberance sometimes went a little too far. One night, in a song and dance number, a member of the chorus accidentally kicked off his shoe. It went flying across the stage and hit the announcer in the cheek breaking his cheekbone. He left the ship for a few days to recover.

By late June, I was in three numbers: "Look Ahead", the opening, which was a group song and dance, "Let All Things Now Living" and a duet with Ralph Church, the Third Purser, singing "16 Tons". The duet didn't work very well because our voices didn't match, his being a tenor and mine a bass. His style reminded me of a sick hillbilly and he clutched badly. This, plus my own inexperience, screwed us up and the duet was quickly dropped from the show!

The summer's big event, over Labor Day weekend, was when both the *North* and *South American* rendezvoused at Mackinac Island and the two crews put on a joint show at the Grand Hotel. The show for the passengers of the ships, hotel guests and locals was a competitive affair with a trophy going to the ship's crew that put on the best show. Historically, the *South American* always won the competition, but we felt that this was going to be our year.

By mid-July, we began rehearsing the show. We hoped to put on the production of "Down in the Valley" but were concerned that the rights might cost too much. Joyce and Wayne would star and I was pleasantly surprised to learn that the only other major male role was mine.

In a few days, it was confirmed that the show would be too costly to put on so we decided to keep our Variety Show format. The Director put me on the Committee that assigned various people to the various numbers. That was a tough job because we had to manage both the level of talent and the watch schedules to ensure that rehearsals could be held.

The show Director approached me and asked if I'd be interested in singing a solo. That seemed to be an honor so I asked him what song he had in mind. He replied, "I Got Plenty of Nuttin'". I thought that was appropriate so I agreed. I sang the number every Sunday night for the rest of the summer. I found that, if I went out and smiled and looked as though I knew how to sing, the audience was able to grin and bear the performance.

The show Director pulled me aside and asked me to be in yet another number, "Standing On The Corner". While this was flattering, it meant more time rehearsing instead of going ashore for R&R. A glutton for punishment, I consented.

We had quite a setback in mid-August. After the Crew Show, the band engaged in a poker game and ended up playing until 4 AM. They managed to sleep through our stopover in Cleveland and were summarily fired!

With a new band and lots more rehearsals, we were finally ready for our Labor Day show at the Grand Hotel. Surprisingly, it went really well and the audience gave us a standing ovation. After the show, I actually had someone come up to me and compliment my singing. Wow! However, the judges were not as impressed and, once again, we suffered the ignominy of losing to the *South American.*

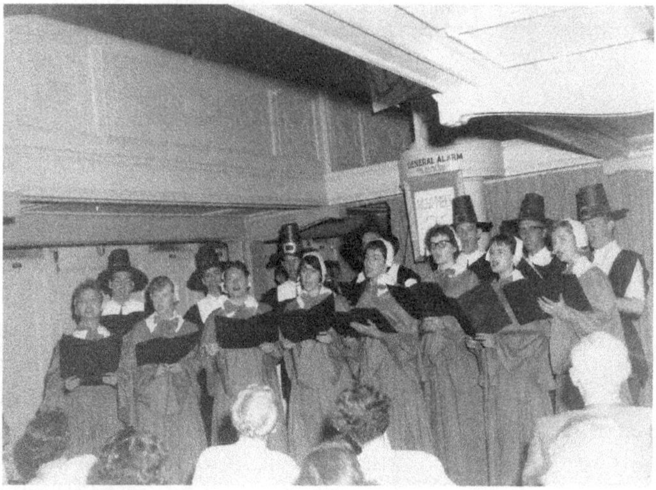

Figure 10: Pilgrim Number (Author Second From Right-Back Row)

Figure 11: At The Grand Hotel, Mackinac Island--

Figure 12: Chorus--W4IWH

Figure 13: The Author With the Lead Singer of the Crew Show

CHAPTER FOUR

LAKE ERIE RESCUE

The shallowest of the Great Lakes, Lake Erie is known for its rough waters. In a blow, the shallow Lake never has a chance to build up the big rolling seas that are found on the oceans. Thus, a short, steep chop builds up that can be dangerous to mariners.

Around 10 PM one evening in August, during a Lake Erie blow, I was on the fantail and heard the engine slow down. I sensed something wrong and as I peered over the side, I saw the safety valve blow to release steam and then, our emergency generator on the radio shack started. I ran up to investigate and discovered we had run across a disabled, small pleasure boat.

The pilothouse was in a panic because, when they turned on their big radar, they blew a fuse, leaving them completely in the dark without power or steering control. The situation was remedied and they got spotlights on the boat.

The boat appeared to be about 25 feet long but it had no real topsides for protection. It was a typical small fishing boat. The boat was bobbing like a cork in the very rough weather. Previously, they dropped an anchor to head the boat into the waves and, if it wasn't for this, I think the boat would have rolled over and capsized. She had three seats consisting of planks between the two sides. To my horror, there were three men aboard and each one was wrapped around a seat hugging it for dear life. The boat was near vertical at times and clearly these men were in imminent danger.

Phil, as the Chief Radio Officer, took over control of the radios. I contacted the pilothouse to ask what I could do, and they asked me to operate the large searchlight on the stern of the *North*. A narrow walkway led from the radio shack back to the stern and I began to move slowly along it. Our ship was lurching in the waves and, suddenly, I lost my balance and began to fall overboard. Fortunately, I caught myself on the railing at my feet and then proceeded to the searchlight.

Phil called the Coast Guard stations around Lake Erie on our radio equipment for ten minutes without an answer. Were they asleep? Finally, he contacted Coast Guard station, NMD-Cleveland, on Morse code. Phil was trying to get them to place a telephone call to the Erie Coast Guard to alert them to the situation. However, the operator at NMD had trouble copying the code from Phil. That was not Phil's fault since he was an excellent, professional radio operator.

Captain Picard maneuvered the *North American* upwind of the small boat so we shielded it from the strong winds and waves. The people aboard were now out of immediate danger. Also, the pilothouse contacted two other ships, the Jos. S. Scobelle and the T. J. McCarthy, by short range FM radio. These ships changed course to relieve us so that we could continue on and meet our passengers' needs

Phil continued trying to contact the Erie Coast Guard with no luck. He did not fare much better with the operator at NMD but finally felt he got through to them and hoped that they would relay the situation to the Erie Coast Guard.

The Scobelle arrived and took over the situation so we went on our way. Just after midnight, while on my watch, the Scobelle radioed it had the three men aboard and was towing their boat to Erie. I felt greatly relieved that three human lives had been saved and hoped that they appreciated their good luck that the *North* had happened upon them.

All of a sudden, Erie Coast Guard came to life and decided to send out a Coast Guard cutter. The guy at the Coast Guard base station started calling the 40-footer with an excited voice that sounded as though he was handling emergency traffic for the Titanic! However, he couldn't seem to contact the 40-footer and so we were concerned that the boat would circle the area for hours while the men were safely on their way to Erie.

Finally, around 2 AM, the Coast Guard cutter stumbled across the Scobelle and announced that they were ready to take over the rescue mission. The captain of the Scobelle politely suggested that they return home as everything was under control.

CHAPTER FIVE

LIFE ONBOARD

We led a dual life onboard: One half involved our interaction with the passengers and the other was our life with our fellow crewmembers. The passengers were typically very nice and treated us well but there were occasionally some real characters. And so it was with the crew. Most of the college kids got along well with each other but there were sometimes tensions with the old hands onboard. Some of these experienced seamen were misfits who had drifted into the marine life to escape problems onshore and some had pasts that were best forgotten.

Many of the passengers were onboard to celebrate a birthday or an anniversary or who just wanted to enjoy the fresh air and laid back life on a ship. Already in a good mood, these people were a delight to serve. Others seemed to come for the express purpose of getting drunk and/or eating until they could hardly walk. A few were just plain ornery.

In addition to our regular cruise schedule, we would sometimes do a charter for a group. The Grand Rapids Chamber of Commerce was one such charter and was memorable for the amount of booze consumed. A few members of this rowdy group somehow found their way into the female crew quarters and they were shown the door in no uncertain terms.

And then there were the Episcopalian ministers who would work hard all day long in meetings but sure knew how to party at night. Our bandleader suggested to us that any one of them could drink us right under the table!

One of the more fascinating couples to come onboard was the "Hollywood" couple and they created quite a stir. The male half was very suave with a mustache and goatee. He looked like a caricature of a Hollywood producer, and all the girls were taken with him. The female half of the couple was very young and beautiful! She wore leopard skin outfits on deck and very low cut gowns to the dining room. She smoked from a long cigarette holder and looked like the producer's paramour. Wherever they went, they put on quite a show and seemed to like the commotion they caused. Regarding the girl—all the boys were definitely taken with her!

My main interaction with the passengers was when they wanted to make a radiotelephone call to someone on shore or to send a telegram. These were relatively uneventful once the passenger learned how to use the radiotelephone. Unlike today's cell phones that allow speaking and listening at the same time, the radiotelephone was a one-way channel. To speak, a button was pressed and during that time you could not hear the other person. Conversely, when listening, anything you said would not be transmitted to the other person. When you finished speaking, you said, "Over".

Most people grasped the technique quickly. However, one customer gave me quite a tough time. I think he was out of his head or drunk or both. He wanted a call put through to a doctor in Chicago. I instructed him over and over on the phone's use but he couldn't understand. He finally just stood there and screamed "hello, hello, hello!!" while pushing the push-to-talk switch on and off rapidly.

Finally, he held the switch down and said the following: "They said 'All ashore who are going ashore' and so the Captain, the Radio Operator and I are the only ones left. It's very cold and even Mr. Webster, the big shot, is very inhospitable. They're all confused because they ran up on a sandbar."

He ranted and raved after the call was over about paying outlandish prices for the call. The call lasted for 18 minutes and the shore station, WLC, charged us for only 3 but he was still unhappy. As he left, he opened the door but didn't hold on to it and it caught the breeze and smashed against the railing, showering glass for 20 feet straight back. It's lucky no one was sunning there.

As for the crew, some of them, like the mates, deck hands and engine room personnel, were seasoned mariners but much of the crew was comprised of college age, young adults serving as waitresses, busboys, bellmen, etc. This made for a fun time in the off hours whether it was hanging out on the ship or exploring on shore leave. And, of course, "chemistry" ran its course through the crew and there were many summer romances.

The girls lived in a section of the ship down low that we called "The Harem". The boys lived in an area called, "The Flicker". The crew also had access to the Fantail, which was the lowest deck on the stern of the ship and to the Poop Deck, which was the highest deck on the stern where we could sunbathe when off duty. Access to the crew quarters from the fantail was through a hole in the deck and down a ladder.

The Fantail is where some of the crew would congregate at night to relax, play cards and perhaps have a drink. We also had a radio and could listen to programs like the Patterson/Johansson fight and Kennedy getting the Democrat's nomination for President. We would frequently play card games like "Down the River".

We had a real character on board, Mike Calabash, who was one of the AB's (Able Bodied Seaman...a deckhand). He was drunk most of the time but also could recite poetry at length and had many fun tales to tell. However, swear words comprised the bulk of his vocabulary. Three excerpts from my diary relate a few tales about Mike:

"Mike crawled out of his hole on the fantail roaring drunk tonight. He swore and started cutting up as usual and then grabbed Kay's pocketbook, Ben Hur, and threw it off the fantail. He really got would up and started quoting poetry and finally swore at all the officers he hated, called the ship an insane asylum and a three ring circus, and threw his work gloves overboard saying "I quit!" and then instructing the gloves to bring the book back!"

"Ralph was on the fantail and was necking with Lorrie. His hat was laid down beside him. With a little coaxing, Mike turned his talents on attempting to throw the cap overboard. He made several attempts but he never could quite steal it, much to the delight of the spectators. He finally gave another burst of swearing and yelled "Good night!" and disappeared down the hole to the Flicker. He is tanked up all the time and is quite funny."

"Mike made himself a cowboy lasso and tried to 'Corral himself a gal' but without too much success. He said he could never be a cowboy though because he was riding a horse once and told it to go hard starboard but the horse became confused at this and threw him. He finally got mad as usual and cussed everyone out and then crawled back down his hole!"

My relationship with Joyce continued to blossom and Mackinac Island became a place where we shared some special moments. One evening, we nearly missed the boat. Joyce and I set out to see a natural bridge that some other crewmembers told us about. We walked for half an hour and were about ready to give up when we saw some rustic steps up the side of a heavily wooded sheer cliff. We decided to explore, so we climbed up about 2-300 feet on a washed out old trail and finally came to some shelters and a cement runway that led out to the natural bridge.

We watched ships sail past and enjoyed the evening. Suddenly, we realized that the ship was going to sail in about 55 minutes!

We started down the path but soon became lost. At one point, I was moving down the path and my left leg fell through a hole in the path. I dropped to my right knee and, fortunately, caught myself. By climbing up and down the cliff and backtracking whenever we were lost, we made it down the cliff with a half hour to go. We ran part of the way back to the ship and made it with only 15 minutes to spare.

Joyce was very popular. Everyone admired her for her outstanding performance as the lead singer in the Crew Show. But on top of that, she was just a really nice, fun person.

Some of her friends and I celebrated her 21st birthday by setting 25 yellow roses, her favorite flower, inside the Harem door. When the girls discovered the flowers, it caused quite a stir. Then, when Phil went down to breakfast, he delivered three fake radio telegrams to her including one signed by: "Mr. Lucking, Mr. Goebel, Mr. Dow, Capt. Picard and the crew of the North and South American". We had shore leave so, at noon, Joyce and I went to Niagara Falls, New York along with some of our friends. At dinner ashore that night, Joyce experienced her first taste of champagne. She got a little tipsy, but she liked it.

While Joyce was very special to me, our relationship posed a bit of a dilemma because I also had a sometime girlfriend, Karen, from college who lived near Chicago. One day, Karen came down to see the ship with my mom and dad, and we went to the Chicago Athletic Club for lunch. Then we toured the ship. We also met a fraternity brother on the dock, as the ship was getting ready to leave. He wanted a picture of Karen and me, so I put my arm around her and he took it. Then, I looked up and there was Joyce on the poop deck looking very puzzled. I said goodbye to Karen and rushed to the poop deck whereupon Joyce and I put our arms around each other. Then, I looked down and there was Karen looking very puzzled! I had some explaining to do!

One of the highlights of the summer occurred when my parents came aboard for a cruise to Mackinac Island. I arranged with Mr. Beauregard, the Chief Steward, to sit at Joyce's table with my parents. Usually, I would sit at the Captain's Table area, which consisted of two round tables on a slightly elevated platform. One was for the Captain, Mates and department Chiefs and the other was for lesser mortals like the Second and Third Radio Operators.

After dinner, I brought my parents to the fantail so they could experience my crew life. Joyce and I played bridge with them and we beat them. They got the full crew experience when Mike made an appearance. He was his usual drunk self and got into a fistfight with McGee. He exclaimed that he would have thrown McGee overboard "except for the wire, retaining fence that stopped me!" I think my parents must have wondered what on earth their son was involved with!

Figure 14: The Author and His Parents Dine at one of the two Captain's Tables

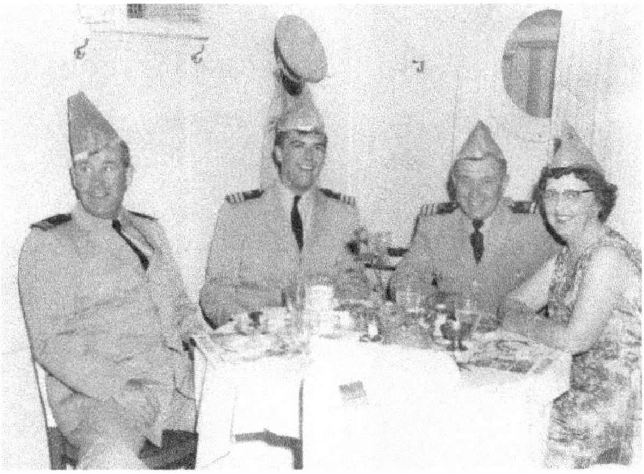

Figure 15: Cousin Phil (Second from Left) Dines with Captain Picard & Wife & the Second Mate

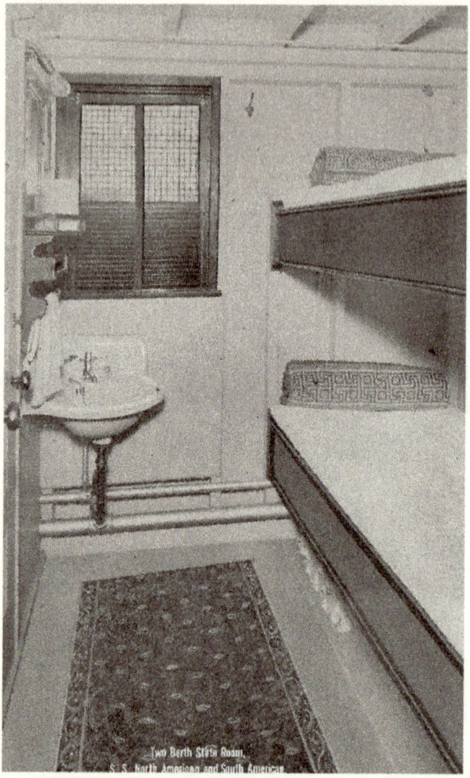

Figure 16: Typical Cabin--W4IWH

Figure 17: Band Provides Entertainment As We Leave the Dock and for the Crew Show--Ogdensburg Journal

Figure 18: Dining Room Section--BGSU

Figure 19: Social Hall--W4IWH

CHAPTER SIX

AGROUND IN THE ST. LAWRENCE RIVER

June 24 began our second trip up the St. Lawrence River. I was really looking forward to seeing the Thousand Islands area again and going through the locks up to Quebec City. However, the morning was rainy and the forecast was ominous with gale force winds being predicted. The river was full of whitecaps and the locks up ahead were closed because of the gale.

Ogdensburg, New York was our first planned stop. This burg was a typical riverfront town with a population of around 10,000. The earliest settlement in Ogdensburg dates back to 1749 when the celebrated Sulpician missionary Father Picquet founded his mission on the banks of the St. Lawrence at the mouth of the Oswegatchie River. The area was the northern terminus of an original Indian trail that ran from the Mohawk Valley to the St. Lawrence. The City developed into an important port of entry and railroad center during the 19th and early 20th centuries, with extensive trade in lumber and grains.

The landing was tricky because a sandbar in the middle of the river created an obstacle. To reach the dock, the ship went up the left hand side of the river heading Northeast until it reached the top of the sandbar. At that point, she needed to make a U-turn and go down a narrow channel to the dock. The ship would be landing with the gale force winds hitting the starboard side, thus pushing it towards the nearby shore.

Captain Picard made the approach in good shape but, as he turned the ship around the top of the sandbar into the gale, he overcorrected for the wind thus pointing the ship directly at the sandbar. The ship shuddered as he ran onto the sandbar at full speed!

This was rather embarrassing because the Executive Vice President of the Georgian Bay Line, Mr. Goebel, was on shore waiting to join the ship for the cruise up the Seaway. Also, an experienced Seaway Pilot was on board, George Woods of Ogdensburg, whose job was to see us safely up the river and the Seaway. There must have been a lot of finger pointing in the pilothouse during this escapade!

It was 4 PM, and I was off watch at the time. Ogdensburg provided some nice tennis courts right by the dock ,and I was in my tennis clothes waiting to go ashore. I stood in the main lobby area along with about a hundred passengers, all waiting anxiously to go ashore. I felt the ship run aground and immediately went back to the radio shack. There, Phil was at the operating position helping with the emergency radio traffic.

The good news was that there was little apparent major damage...we were not sinking. The bad news, which we didn't realize at the time, was that we would be stuck for another six days. There was nothing to do but to continue with daily life aboard the ship until we could be pulled free. Dinner was served normally. followed by the Crew Show entertainment for the passengers.

By evening, quite a crowd had gathered at the waterfront to gawk at our predicament. We were only a hundred yards or so offshore so we could clearly see each other. The local radio station began interrupting regular programming with "bulletins" that were amusing because of the many inaccuracies they contained.

At 9 PM, a large tug came over from the Canadian side of the river and tried to pull us off but we didn't budge. The radio log at 11 PM read, "On watch, sunk at Ogdensburg"--a feeble attempt at a joke. At midnight, as I came on watch, Mr. Goebel brought a VHF radio on board for use in communicating with the Ogdensburg Police Department. My instructions were to call them every half hour for messages. I thought Mr. Goebel was rather calm considering all that was going on.

The following is a day-by-day account of this adventure based on the notes in a diary that I kept (The unabridged diary is contained in the Appendix):

June 25 at 5:30 AM two tugs arrived: The America and the Robinson Bay. They connected cables to the ship as big around as your arm to pull it. When this didn't work, they tried to push the ship off the sandbar. Then another tug, Miss Lana, joined in the fun and there was much pulling and pushing. Nothing worked...we were really stuck. The problem was that the gale had subsided. While it was blowing, water was being pushed up the river and the water level rose. When the gale ended, the water flowed back making the river lower.

The radio room was unbelievably busy. We were constantly making announcements over the Public Address System. Then the passengers wanted to send messages to friends and family that they were ok. Then they wanted to cancel reservations ahead and make new ones. And we were also helping with all the communications related to the ship issues. Whew!

The locals enjoyed all of this immensely. The paper ran front-page headlines, "North American Runs Aground Off Rutland Dock-347 Passengers Spend Night On Sand Bar" with three large photos of the ship. We were aground only about a hundred yards offshore which was rather embarrassing; it was also frustrating since shore was so near and yet so far away. There were dozens of people in small boats buzzing around the ship waving and cavorting. One joker in a small outboard skiff, offered us a line to give us at tow!

Conditions on the ship began to deteriorate as water began to run out. Toilets were clogging and began backing up. Fortunately, a ferry arrived around 11 AM with a load of water and this helped for a while.

By early afternoon, a ferry arrived to take 62 passengers off the ship and brought them to Prescott where they took the train to Montreal. Thus, they missed the locks but were able to continue with their vacation plans while we dealt with the ship. The remaining passengers stayed onboard hoping that the *North* would be off the sandbar quickly so that the trip could resume and they could see the locks.

At 4:30 PM, the ferry arrived again and took many passengers ashore so they could explore Ogdensburg. It returned at 7 PM. The crew was not allowed off the ship so they were going a little crazy by this time. By later in the evening, water began running low again. Mr. Collie, the Chief Steward, told the waitresses that they might be laid off for a week or so while the ship goes into dry dock to repair the hull.

June 26 saw the arrival of more tugs including the Melanie Fair, a huge sea-going tug manned by a British crew. The tugs on station by the end of the day and their horsepower were:

Melanie Fair--2000 HP
Salvage Monarch—1400 HP
Salvage Prince—500 HP
Robinson Bay—1400 HP
America—1000 HP
Miss Lana—1250 HP

In addition, the Monarch and Prince were equipped with special anchors that they secure in the mud and then use big bow winches to get extra pull. Unfortunately, more pulling and pushing today resulted in no movement of the ship so the captains of the various vessels involved spent the afternoon planning for a coordinated effort tomorrow.

We announced over the PA system that the passengers could take a bus tour to the Eisenhower and Snell Locks in the morning. Many people took the cruise just to see these locks so they were happy with these arrangements. If the tugs can't free the ship tomorrow, we were told the passengers would be sent home and dredging would start, which could take 3 to 5 days.

Water was replenished tonight and both Ben and I crowded into our small room and took dry showers. I really felt good for the first time in a couple of days. We hoarded drinking water in two glasses and a paper cup, and found that we could wash our hands by turning on an auxiliary fire hose outlet at my fire station on the side of the radio shack. Passenger morale was still ok but the crew sure could use some time ashore!

June 27: The Eisenhower Lock made an announcement that the SS Invar was aground below the Snell Lock so apparently we weren't the only ones to run into difficulties.

The Ogdensburg Journal's headline read, "North American Still Stuck Aground on Sand Bar--Tugs Fail to Budge Ship Carrying 347". A front-page picture showed a huge traffic jam near the docks as people from all over came to survey the ship's plight.

An article in the paper reported on the accident as follows:

"The Captain of the North American, Russell Picard, not the pilot, Captain George Woods of Ogdensburg, was in charge of the ship when she was coming into harbor. Captain Woods had turned her over to Captain Picard in mid-channel in the St. Lawrence.

The ship was traveling against a strong wind. It was hugging the sandbar because of the wind, which threatened to drive it too close to the shore. The pilot warned the captain that the ship was getting dangerously close to the channel marker, but for some reason, before anything could be done, the ship went aground.

A separate article reported that Captain Woods issued the following statement:

'On June 24 when abreast of the lights of Ogdensburg at mid-stream, I as pilot turned the ship over to the captain, Russell Picard. The captain, the master of the ship, is in command at all times. While making the turn into the Ogdensburg Harbor I was in the wheelhouse. The ship was coming along fine, we made the turn in good shape. We got close to the red buoy and I advised the Captain three times that he should come left. The Captain was apparently holding the ship up for drift.

I have no authority to say anything to the Captain. He is in command of the ship; the pilot is on board in advisory capacity.

Captain Picard has been a skipper for many years. He has made several voyages to Ogdensburg over the years. Captain Picard knows the local harbor quite well. The weather conditions he was operating under were quite bad'"

The new tug from London worked with the others all day but without success. The problem was that the *North American* drew about 17-1/2 feet of water but the depth of water where she sat is about 10 feet so she was really high and dry

June 28: The tugs tried their all yesterday but the ship didn't budge. At this point, Captain Picard appeared quite haggard. The new plan was to start dredging in the morning and rumors are circulating that the ship may go into dry dock for a while. It was unclear whether the radio operators were going or staying.

By this time, we became international news. I received reports that papers around the US and Canada were running articles about our predicament. The Toronto Star's headlines were typical saying, "Tugs Fail To Free Ship but Passengers Still Happy".

I continued to be incredibly busy on my watches with sending messages and arranging for buses with the police. I was exhausted and so was everyone else. We were minus water all day but finally got some in the evening. I never knew how good it could feel to wash my face!

The Britishers off the Melanie Fair were very smart and proper and their accent was very interesting. The man in charge was Scottish and very professional.

The passengers left in the morning. Most crew were working about half of their regular hours so there was almost a festive air aboard the ship. It seemed like the feeling one has when finals are over and you're about ready to go home. No one really knew what was going to be done with the crew but everyone expected an announcement soon. The weather was still sunny and nice and morale was good all things considered.

Tonight, the crew got shore leave for the first time since June 23. Most went wild and got drunk at Oscar's. I preferred to take the ferry to Prescott and explored an old fort. I took a shower for the first time in many days.

June 29: The Steward's Department, Pursers and other non-essential crew were laid off this afternoon. Only about 17 will remain including the three radio operators.

The dredges started work this afternoon and dredged a ditch along our port or shore side. They worked around the clock to free the ship. The new plan was to dig two large pits (Deadmen) on shore and then fill them with lumber and concrete. These Deadmen will become anchors for cables from the tugs. Two tugs, one near the *North*'s bow and the other near her stern will then attach cables to the *North* from their sterns. Each tug has big bow winches and these will be connected to the Deadmen ashore. A bulldozer on shore with a cable to the ship will also pull. Two tugs will push on our starboard side. The final two tugs will each hold a bow line or a stern line to control the ship once she floats free.

June 30: In the morning, with the Deadmen ashore complete, it was time to execute on the new plan. The tugs went to their positions and we filled with excitement and anticipation. When the signal to begin was given, the tugs gave their boats and winches full power and then I heard a "crack"! A cable as big around as my forearm snapped and went whipping around. It was lucky that it didn't kill someone!

The tug reattached a cable and the procedure was repeated. This time, the ship tilted a little but the Deadmen ashore were torn up from their pits and we broke a bit in the bow! We were still stuck!

After discussions among the tugboat captains and Captain Picard, the decision was made to build stronger Deadmen on shore and try again. About 4 PM, the bigger Deadmen were complete and the tugs and bulldozer started pulling again. I took a sighting on a bridge to our stern and at first, I couldn't tell whether we were actually moving or just listing but soon it was evident that the stern was swinging toward shore. The stern moved very slowly but at 4:38 PM we finally became buoyant.

The Melanie Fair, which held a line to our bow, took off immediately but the cable snapped. There was a strong on-shore breeze and we started blowing ashore. We dropped our anchor and came out of any immediate danger. Meanwhile the Melanie Fair was in reverse and ran over the broken cable. Luckily, it didn't snag in the propeller for if it had, she would have blown ashore onto the rocks. Finally, everyone got straightened out and we made it to the city dock on our own power.

It was a strange but pleasant feeling to be under way again. The hull of the North was all dirty, scratched and dented but there was no apparent major damage. Tomorrow the Coast Guard will inspect her and then the *North* will sail for Buffalo where it will start the season on Tuesday, July 5. In celebration, I had a beer and saw a show in the evening.

July 1: The Ogdensburg Journal's headline reported, "North American Freed After 6 Days On Sand Bar". The paper continued to try to establish the facts around the grounding and provided the following analysis:

"According to the ship's reports, the wind was blowing at about 34 miles per hour with gusts up to 45 miles per hour when the North American went aground. Captain Picard, who was handling the ship at the time, was faced with two problems, one of the sand bar and the other the heavy rocks along the shore. With 347 passengers aboard, Captain Picard had to take every precaution to avoid hitting any rocks. In maneuvering his ship around, the veteran skipper apparently hung to close to the bar. When the ship first struck, it looked as if she might be removed without much trouble, but then the wind went down, the water dropped about 12 inches and the ship settled into the sand-covered clay."

Today the Coast Guard inspected the ship and the crew welded part of her bow back on where a chock was ripped out. Also there was much activity scrubbing and repainting part of the hull. She looked as good as new!

The only other damage was to the egos of some waitresses. The Englishmen on the Melanie Fair charmed several of them and they ended up living aboard for a few days. Mr. Collie did not approve and he summarily fired them.

July 2: The *North American* sailed for Buffalo today amid much horn blowing and cheering and waving from the natives. Marty, the Social Director, handed out the usual streamers to the handful of maids and crewmembers who were on hand and Ben played some march music over the PA. to take the place of our band. Capt. Picard took the flying bridge with a big grin on his face and then we left the thriving metropolis of Ogdensburg, NY.

No one on board was too upset over leaving. We probably disrupted the whole economy of the burg due to the large expenditures made by the passengers and crew. Their paper sounded very sad to see us leave.

Figure 20: Five Tugs and a Dredge Try to Free The North American--Ogdensburg Journal

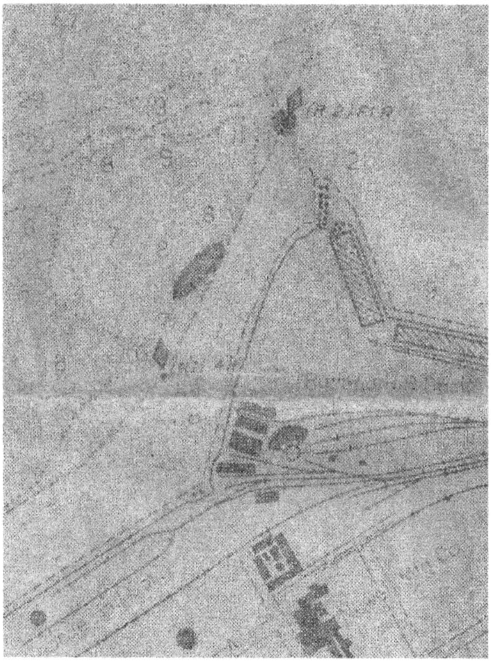

Figure 21: Marine Chart Showing Channel and Sandbar--Ogdensburg Journal

Figure 25: Tugs Pushing and Pulling--Ogdensburg Journal

Figure 26: Traffic Jam of Sightseers--Ogdensburg Journal

Figure 27: North American Lists to Port as Tugs Push and Pull--Ogdensburg Journal

CHAPTER SEVEN

LAKE MICHIGAN STORM

Lake Michigan is another treacherous body of water. About 300 miles long, the Lake is almost half the distance from Newport, Rhode Island to Bermuda. On Northerly or Southerly winds, the Lake can build up offshore-type conditions. If the wind is from the West or East, a very steep chop can build quickly as the wind whips off the shore. Midwestern weather is notoriously unpredictable and frontal passages frequently are accompanied by gale force or storm force winds. Chicago is not named the "Windy City" for nothing.

After completing a charter trip for the Grand Rapids Chamber of Commerce, the *North American's* itinerary called for an overnight trip to Chicago to board passengers for a trip to Mackinac Island. The trip was a deadhead, meaning that there were no passengers aboard, which was good because the forecast was for stormy weather.

The ship left Holland, Michigan in the evening so the major part of the trip would be on my watch. I went to the galley and ate a big sandwich, as was my custom before going on watch. The ship was rocking and rolling, and I had to hold on to the railings tightly as I made my way up to the radio shack. I could hardly open the door to the shack because of the wind.

As I continued on my watch, the weather conditions worsened. The ship was rolling heavily, spray was blowing back from the bow to the stern and the ship was shuddering as she slammed into the waves. The wind was shrieking like a stuck pig.

Books flew out of the bookshelves and the fan tore off the wall, narrowly missing my head. The storm intensified and I could no longer sit in the folding chair at the radio operating position; I held onto the desk to keep from falling over.

My mental state changed from concern to outright fear. Never before had I experienced anything like this and the creaks and groans from the ship sent shivers up and down my spine.

I began staring at a small calendar on the wall with a hole in it that was placed over a nail. The calendar was going back and forth with the ship's roll. Back and forth, back and forth, left to right, right to left...I became hypnotized.

To occupy my mind and to focus on something other than the extreme outside conditions, I would wait for the ship to take a really big roll and then mark where the calendar went so that I could measure the angle of the rolls we were taking. Measuring these marks later with a protractor showed that we were taking 20-35 degree rolls! I'm not sure what the ship was designed for but we had to be at the limits of stability.

Focusing on the calendar instead of watching the horizon, a standard procedure to avoid seasickness, was a big mistake. Sure enough, I noticed that the big sandwich I ate before coming on watch was not sitting well in my stomach! I began to feel seasick. I'd never been seasick before even though I'd been through some rough stuff, not only on the *North,* but also cruising all over Lake Michigan on my parents' small powerboat. This was not good! Sure enough, after fighting the seasickness for a while, I struggled to open the door to the radio shack and made my offering to King Neptune. This storm was one of only two times in my life that I've been seasick.

We continued to lurch and slam into the waves for the next several hours. As we neared Chicago, we approached the lee shore where the waves were not as large and the wind began to abate a bit. Finally, we entered the channel behind the breakwater and entered the locks. Had there been ground to kiss, I would have been on my knees.

Later, I spoke with the Third Mate and he told me that he was seeing winds up to 70 MPH...Hurricane force...until the anemometer blew off. He confessed that he was also afraid and that he thought the windows in the pilothouse would blow in. This storm was one of the few times in my life that I really thought I was going to die.

CHAPTER EIGHT

THE DETROIT WHARF

The weather always seemed to worsen whenever we went down the St. Clair River, across Lake St. Clair and then docked at Detroit. It became a source of much discussion and speculation as to whether the Gods were against us. We did not look forward to our time there.

The wharf was weather-beaten and dark. Every twenty feet or so, a group of eight pilings, arranged in a 2 X 4 pattern, held up the wharf. Essentially telephone poles, these pilings were also weather-beaten and dark. The pilings looked scruffy from the many run-ins they had with the ships that docked there.

The current in the Detroit River was decent, peaking at 1.5-2 MPH. This proved challenging for the *North American*. Docking at the wharf was pretty easy. The ship went down current, turned around and then eased its way onto the wharf by sort of "crabbing" over.

However, leaving the wharf was more challenging. The procedure involved leaving the wharf going backwards and then pointing the stern into the middle of the river. Then, with a full starboard rudder and full forward power, the ship would make a "swoop" by the wharf and be on its way. The secret to a successful maneuver was to get far enough out into the middle of the river so that the "swoop" back cleared the wharf.

One day, I was on watch as we left Detroit. Leaving the dock was perfectly normal and we began backing into the river. Suddenly, Captain Picard gave the ship full throttle. "Uh oh" I thought...this is not going to go well because we were not far enough out into the channel to begin our "swoop" back.

We came charging back into the wharf at full speed and I braced myself. People on the dock began to back up and then run. Sure enough, we grazed the wharf and caught a group of eight pilings in one of our port cargo hatches. There was a loud cracking sound as we snapped these pilings as though they were matchsticks.

Fortunately, no one was hurt (except for the Captain's pride) but the cargo hatch was severely bent. For the rest of the summer, whenever we came back to Detroit, there were eight, white, shiny, new pilings on the wharf to mark our misadventure

CHAPTER NINE

FLYING SAUCER

I liked my 12-4 watch. In the afternoons, the radio shack was busy and I enjoyed helping the passengers with their communications. The early morning hours were peaceful and quiet and I could enjoy the views from one of the highest points on the ship. I spent many nights gazing at the sky watching the incredible Northern Lights while meteors streaked across the sky. This watch also allowed me to participate in the Crew Show and to hang with other crewmembers on the ship's fantail after dinner and the show.

One night, while making my sandwich before going on watch, I looked out the galley porthole and saw that the moon was glistening on the still water. I really looked forward to my watch and anticipated an uneventful, peaceful and beautiful night.

I climbed the steps to the top of the ship where the radio shack was located and marveled at the beauty of the moonlit night. On the passenger's Promenade Deck, I passed a couple of passengers who were heaving their dinner over the side. It never ceased to amaze me that people could get seasick on a perfectly still night with essentially no movement of the boat!

As I came on watch, I ate my sandwich and checked all the radios. Everything was in order and the bands were dead quiet.

I stood in the doorway, leaning up against the frame and looked over at the Michigan shoreline. We left Mackinac Island a few hours before so we could still see the shore about 5 miles away and the lights on shore were twinkling. Over my head and behind me was a full moon up in the sky. The moon acted like a spotlight and the moonlight on the water was dancing. It was one of those moments when you are just happy to be alive and communing with nature.

Suddenly, I froze. In the distance about 45 degrees off our stern (the ship's stern quarter), was a small, bright shimmering object coming slowly at us. It was thin on the edges with a round "hump" in the middle. "A FLYING SAUCER!" It slowly undulated up and down as it approached and then suddenly, went straight up and disappeared.

I was stunned! Did I really see that? YES I DID! I debated calling the Third Mate in the wheelhouse since I thought he would think I was nuts. After agonizing about this for a minute, I thought it was my duty to report what I just saw.

In the radio shack, there was a phone with a direct connection to the wheelhouse. It had a crank on its side that, when turned, rang a bell in the wheelhouse. I hesitated with the phone in hand and then bit the bullet and called the Third Mate. I told him what I saw. Rather than laughing at me, he was very interested and asked for more detail. When I finished he said, "If you see it again, make sure to ring me".

Well, now I was on full alert. My heart was pounding and my mind raced about what the flying saucer was doing here. Would it threaten me? Would it try to capture me? The minutes rolled by with no sign of it again. I remembered a tale that a friend of mine, who lived in the Northwoods of Wisconsin, told me about a flying saucer he had seen and so this all sounded very plausible. Still the minutes kept flying by and there was no further sign of the saucer.

Then all of sudden, I saw it again! THERE IT WAS...THE FLYING SAUCER! I leapt into the radio shack and furiously cranked the phone to the Third Mate. I said, "There it is! There it is! The Flying Saucer!" The Third Mate exclaimed, "Oh yes! I see it too!"

There was silence for a moment as the object approached us all shimmering and undulating. It kept coming and coming until it was near the boat and then went swooping overhead. Then the Mate and I recognized what it was. We said, almost in unison, "It's a damn seagull!"

Sure enough, the gull was just gliding along and the moon over my shoulder was illuminating it making it look just like the textbook drawings of a Flying Saucer. The Mate and I had a good laugh and he was kind enough not to give me a hard time about my stupidity! Had I not seen the seagull the second time, I would swear to this day that flying saucers are real.

CHAPTER TEN

ENDINGS AND BEGINNINGS

Our troubles during the summer of 1960 signaled the beginning of the end for the *North American* and eventually, its sister ship the *SS South American* and the Georgian Bay Lines. The financial hit from the grounding in the St. Lawrence River was a big blow for a company that was already struggling. The impact was not only from the expense involved, but it also hurt the company's reputation.

In 1963, the Canadian Holiday Company of Erie, Pennsylvania purchased the *North* for use in cross-lake service between Erie and Port Dover, Ontario, Canada. However, she was retired in 1964. After several attempts at selling her, she was finally sold at public auction to the Seafarers International Union of North America in1967 for use as a training ship at Piney Point, Maryland.

On September 4, 1967, while the *North American* was being towed to Piney Point, she unexpectedly sank off of Nantucket. The cause of this disaster was never established but there were rumors that the towing company did not close a valve somewhere on the ship and she filled with water during the night and sank. It was a sad end to a glorious ship.

In July 2006, a research team aboard Quest Marine's research vessel *Quest* located the *North American* in about 250 feet of water. Their obsession with finding the ship is related in their 2020 book, "Shallow Waters". The book describes their first sighting of the *North American*:

"The bow's intact and leaning well over to port. Rows of window openings and portholes line the sides of the hull. Inside, the wooden bulkheads separating the staterooms have rotted away leaving sinks attached to the steel plating. Both anchors are still housed in their respective Hawse pipes. The windless is still in place under the foredeck. A large nylon hawser, an artifact of the last voyage, hangs down from the bow and extends out into the sand on the starboard side. Pat finds the remains of the crew's shower up in the bow. The floor's lined with octagon-shaped black and white tiles."

For those of us who served aboard her, she will always hold a special place in our hearts. We loved her. We were very lucky to experience the adventures described in this book as the Great Lakes Passenger Ship era came to a close.

Cousin Phil Shuman joined Motorola but continued to substitute aboard the *North* and *South American* during his vacations. After a few years, he moved to St. Croix in the US Virgin Islands. Initially, he developed a business to service communications equipment and radar aboard ships in the Caribbean. True to form, he became the "go to" guy for ships ranging from large tankers and cruise ships to private mega-yachts. Later, he joined AT&T where he was responsible for the international undersea communications cables that terminated in St. Croix. Again, his role was to keep the cable systems operating and he served admirably in this endeavor. Phil died in 2015.

Joyce went back to school at St. Olaf's College in Northfield, Minnesota and I returned to Purdue for my senior year. I missed her and decided to hop up to see her one weekend. This was a 7-1/2 hour, 530-mile one-way trip. Not too long after I arrived, it was apparent that the strong relationship we had in the summer had cooled.

However, one ending became another beginning. Seeing Karen in Chicago rekindled my interest in her. Up until then she had been a girl-friend. She attended Butler University about an hour's drive from Purdue and she soon became my girlfriend. However, upon graduation we went to work in different cities and this relationship eventually cooled as well.

For me, the summer was a turning point in my process of growing up. I shouldered a major responsibility and proved to myself that I was capable, even in emergency situations. This was a tremendous boost to my self-confidence. I also demonstrated that I could stand before an audience and perform via participation in the Crew Show, again a confidence booster.

My love of being on the water intensified. I'm an Aquarian and my ancestors are Danish, so there is truly something in my soul and/or my genes that draws me to the water. By my mid-20's, I bought a 23-foot sailboat and taught myself how to sail. Over the years, I've owned a variety of boats, which I've raced and cruised all over New England. I've also sailed offshore to the Caribbean where my wife of 24 years, Gale, and I have cruised by ourselves and with others for many years. And, much to my delight, my daughter, Heather, became a sailor and crewed aboard some of the top racing boats in New England.

I've continued to enjoy ham radio. I've placed well in several operating contests and made contact with 331 of the 340 countries in the world. I'm currently active on the new digital modes such as FT8.

On the *North American*, I learned that I had a pretty decent singing voice and this led to an incident where Gale really fell in love with me. When we were dating, we went to a birthday party at a friend's house. There was a large crowd celebrating the event and the birthday girl hired a piano player to play Broadway tunes. Gale was sitting on a couch talking with a girlfriend. I was talking with the birthday girl near the piano and happened to mention the *North* and the Crew Show. Hearing this, the birthday girl thought it would be great if I sang a song for the crowd. I sure hadn't planned on that and did my best to duck the request! However, she was insistent.

As I surveyed the room, I noticed that there was some pretty heavy drinking going on and, remembering my Crew Show days, I realized that this would work in my favor. As added insurance, I negotiated with the birthday girl to do a duet, hoping that her voice would be louder than mine. We agreed to sing "Some Enchanted Evening" and, again using my Crew Show technique of smiling and pretending that I knew what I was doing, I gave it a go. To my surprise, people stopped talking and listened. At the end, we actually got some applause, much of which I attributed to the booze. In any event, the woman that Gale was talking with on the couch nudged her and said, "He's the one!" And that was, indeed, true as we complete 28 years of a wonderful life together. And I owe it all to my time on the *North!*

CHAPTER ELEVEN

ABOUT THE AUTHOR

Gerry Bay and his wife, Gale, live in Southbury, CT having moved there from Jamestown, RI in 2020. They have four children and ten grandchildren between them.

Gerry was interested in electronics at an early age and became a Ham Radio Operator, WN9OHO, at age 16. He has held a series of call signs including W9OHO, W1GQG, NO1Y and currently, W1XY. Licensed by the Federal Communications Commission, he holds the Extra Class license that is earned by Hams who are the most proficient in Morse code, radio theory and regulations. Currently, he is active on the new digital modes including FT8.

Gerry also grew up in a very water-oriented family. His father was a lieutenant in the Navy and owned several different power boats while he was growing up. The family cruised extensively on Lake Michigan, Green Bay and the Fox River. Later, Gerry owned a number of sailboats on which he raced and cruised New England and the Caribbean. In the 1990's, he owned a Frers 41 named Crescendo and then in the early 2000's, he and Gale sailed to the Caribbean aboard their Hylas 54, Windsong, for a couple of years. They continued to sail the Caribbean aboard a friend's boat for many years.

The marriage of these two interests led him to pursue the ideal summer job of Radio Operator aboard the *SS North American.* Now retired, you can find him enjoying ham radio during the winter and boating during the summer when he's not playing with his grandchildren.

Gerry can be reached at:

416 Tepi Drive
Southbury, CT 06488

CHAPTER TWELVE

OTHER BOOKS BY GERRY BAY

Gerry, and his wife Gale, wrote and published two other books that are available from Amazon in either paperback or Kindle formats.

"Sailing the Caribbean Islands" relates their sailing adventures as they sailed their Hylas 54, Windsong, from Rhode Island to the Caribbean for two years. This book chronicles their adventures and the interesting characters they met along the way. Written as a daily journal, you will feel like you are sailing right along with them as they explore the islands and meet the island folk.

They also wrote "Our St. Lucia". After sailing the Caribbean islands, they fell in love with St. Lucia and purchased an apartment. They spent winters on the island for 15 years and wrote this book to share their insights on where to go and what to do. While common travel guides provide a great overview of the island, this book tells the inside story about what to do when you plan a vacation to this gorgeous island.

APPENDIX

A. Brochure (Bay collection)

Cover

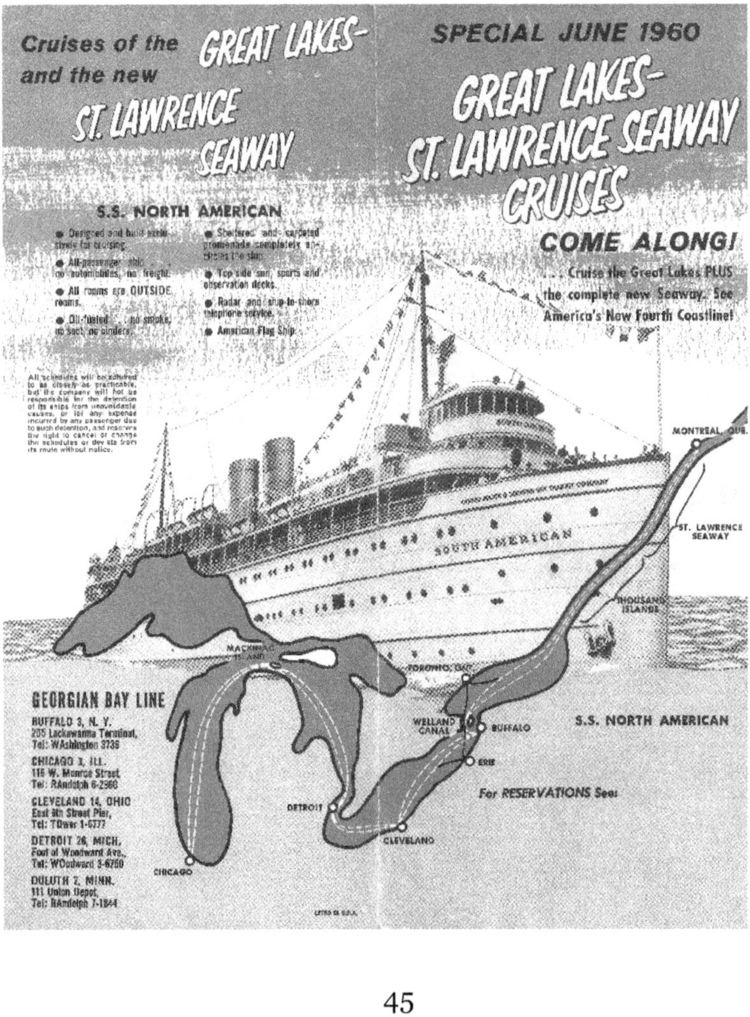

Inside Left

Cruise the Great Lake
Visit Chicago – Mackin
See America's New

JUNE SEAWAY CRUISE #1
S.S. NORTH AMERICAN

PORT	CRUISING AREA	DAY	DATE	TIME
Lv. CHICAGO, ILL.	Lake Michigan	Tues	May 31	11:00 AM
Pass famous Mackinac Straits Bridge		Wed	June 1	8:00 AM
Ar. Mackinac Island		Wed	June 1	10:00 AM
Lv. Mackinac Island	Lake Huron	Wed	June 1	12:00 NOON
Ar. Detroit, Mich.	Detroit River	Thur	June 2	11:00 AM
Lv. DETROIT, MICH.	Lake Erie	Thur	June 2	1:00 PM
Ar. Cleveland, Ohio	Lake Erie	Thur	June 2	10:30 PM
Lv. CLEVELAND, OHIO	Lake Erie	Thur	June 2	11:45 PM
Ar. Erie, Pa.	Lake Erie	Fri	June 3	8:00 AM
Lv. ERIE, PA.	Lake Erie	Fri	June 3	9:30 AM
Enter Welland Canal	Port Colborne, Ont.	Fri	June 3	2:00 PM
Ar. Thorold, Ont. (BUFFALO)	Welland Canal	Fri	June 3	7:00 PM
(Embarkation of Buffalo passengers) Sightseeing trip to Niagara Falls.				
Lv. THOROLD, ONT.	Welland Canal	Fri	June 3	9:30 PM
Leave Welland Canal	Port Weller	Sat	June 4	4:00 AM
Cruise Lake Ontario.				
Pass Cape Vincent, N.Y.	St. Lawrence River	Sat	June 4	4:00 PM
Cruise 1000 Islands of the St. Lawrence				
Ar. Ogdensburg, N.Y.	St. Lawrence River	Sat	June 4	9:00 PM
Lv. OGDENSBURG, N.Y.	St. Lawrence River	Sat	June 4	10:30 PM
Iroquois Lock (6 feet)	Canadian			
Eisenhower Lock (51½ feet)	American			
Snell Lock (51½ feet)	American			
Beauharnois Locks—Upper, 41 ft.; Lower, 41 ft.				
St. Catherine Lock (35 feet)	Canadian			
St. Lambert Lock (15 feet)	Canadian			
Ar. Montreal, Quebec	St. Lawrence River	Sun	June 5	7:00 PM
Lv. MONTREAL, QUEBEC	St. Lawrence River	Mon	June 6	1:00 PM
Ar. Ogdensburg N.Y.	St. Lawrence River	Tue	June 7	10:30 AM
Lv. Ogdensburg N.Y.	St. Lawrence River	Tue	June 7	12:00 NOON
Pass Alexandria Bay, N.Y.	St. Lawrence River			
Pass Thousand Island Bridge	St. Lawrence River			
Pass Cape Vincent, N.Y.	Lake Ontario	Tues	June 7	8:00 PM
Ar. Toronto, Ont.	Lake Ontario	Wed	June 8	8:00 AM
Lv. Toronto, Ont.	Lake Ontario	Wed	June 8	12:00 NOON
Enter Welland Canal	Port Weller, Ont.	Wed	June 8	3:00 PM
Ar. Thorold, Ont. (BUFFALO)	Welland Canal	Wed	June 8	6:00 PM
(Buffalo passengers disembark)				
Lv. Thorold, Ont.	Welland Canal	Wed	June 8	9:00 PM
Ar. Erie, Pa.	Lake Erie	Thur	June 9	11:00 AM
Lv. Erie, Pa.	Lake Erie	Thur	June 9	12:30 PM
Ar. Cleveland, Ohio	Lake Erie	Thur	June 9	8:00 PM
Lv. Cleveland, Ohio	Lake Erie	Thur	June 9	11:59 PM
Ar. Detroit, Mich.	Detroit River	Fri	June 10	8:00 AM
Lv. Detroit, Mich.	Detroit River	Fri	June 10	5:00 PM
Ar. Mackinac Island	Sts. of Mackinac	Sat	June 11	3:00 PM
Lv. Mackinac Island	Sts. of Mackinac	Sat	June 11	9:00 PM
Ar. Chicago, Ill.	Lake Michigan	Sun	June 12	8:00 PM

NOTE: All times shown west of Cleveland are Eastern Standard Time. All times east of Cleveland are Eastern Daylight Saving Time.

ROUND-TRIP RATES—PER PERSON

	DECK "C"	DECK "B"	DECK "A"	BEDROOMS
From—Chicago	$295.00	$330.00	$345.00	$595.00
Detroit	215.00	240.00	255.00	395.00
Cleveland	205.00	230.00	245.00	385.00
Erie	200.00	225.00	240.00	380.00
Buffalo (Thorold)	195.00	220.00	235.00	375.00
*Ogdensburg	125.00	150.00	165.00	295.00

Rates shown above are per person basis two to a room. Meals, transportation, sleeping accommodations, entertainment and Federal Tax on transportation and sleeping accommodations are included. Seaway Lock Tolls on all Roundtrip tickets, $15.00 extra.

*Plus $7.50 Seaway Tolls on Ogdensburg Tickets

RATES — ONE-WAY—TO OR FROM MONTREAL

Chicago	$190.00	$205.00	$217.00	$360.00
Detroit	122.50	137.50	147.50	225.00
Cleveland	117.50	132.50	142.50	220.00
Buffalo (Thorold)	112.50	127.50	137.50	215.00

Plus $7.50 Seaway Tolls on all One-Way Tickets.

Between ports of call there will be plenty of fun afloat

What a marvelous cruise! From Chicago you will sail for 12 delightful days and 12 glorious nights. You'll cruise Lakes Michigan, Huron, Erie, and Ontario; the Straits of Mackinac; the St. Clair, the Detroit and the St. Lawrence Rivers. You'll visit Detroit, Cleveland, Erie and the great metropolis of Canada—Montreal. You'll lock through the tremendous locks of the Welland Canal and the new St. Lawrence Seaway.

Through the Welland Canal connecting Lakes Erie and Ontario

All cabin
are O

SEPTEMBER SEAWAY CRUISE
S.S. SOUTH AMERICAN

Inside Right

... Sail the St. Lawrence Seaway!

c Island – Detroit – Cleveland – Montreal!

ourth Coastline!

Be on deck when your ship cruises the Thousand Islands of the St. Lawrence

You'll sail the 1000 Islands section of the St. Lawrence. And between ports of call you will have the time of your life aboard ship . . . fun, rest, relaxation, gay parties, new friends, entertainment, deck sports, sun bathing, music, dancing and the finest of food to satisfy your sea-going appetite. The cruises of the year! Don't miss them! And bring your camera . . . photo possibilities are unlimited.

d bedrooms
IDE rooms

Rest, relax and enjoy a continuous panorama of scenic beauty

Ask about special color cruise of the S.S. South American to Montreal and Quebec City in early September. Also 12 Great Lakes-St. Lawrence Seaway one-way cruises Chicago to Montreal (either way) aboard ocean-going passenger-cargo ships of the Fjell-Oranje Lines, May thru October.

JUNE SEAWAY CRUISE # 2

S.S. NORTH AMERICAN

PORT	CRUISING AREA	DAY	DATE	TIME
Lv. CHICAGO, ILL.	Lake Michigan	Mon	June 20	11:00 AM
Pass famous Mackinac Straits Bridge		Tues	June 21	8:30 AM
Ar. Mackinac Island		Tues	June 21	9:30 AM
Lv. Mackinac Island	Lake Huron	Tues	June 21	11:30 AM
Ar. Detroit, Mich.	Detroit River	Wed	June 22	9:30 AM
Lv. DETROIT, MICH.	Lake Erie	Wed	June 22	11:30 AM
Ar. Cleveland, Ohio	Lake Erie	Wed	June 22	8:30 PM
Lv. CLEVELAND, OHIO	Lake Erie	Wed	June 22	10:00 PM
Enter Welland Canal	Port Colborne, Ont.	Thur	June 23	9:00 AM
Ar. Thorold, Ont.	Welland Canal	Thur	June 23	2:00 PM
(Embarkation of Buffalo passengers)				
Sightseeing trip to Niagara Falls.				
Lv. THOROLD, ONT. (BUFFALO)	Welland Canal	Thur	June 23	5:00 PM
Leave Welland Canal	Port Weller	Thur	June 23	12:00 MID
Cruise Lake Ontario,				
Pass Cape Vincent, N.Y.	St. Lawrence River	Fri	June 24	12:00 NOON
Pass Clayton, N.Y.	St. Lawrence River	Fri	June 24	2:00 PM
Pass Thousand Island Bridge	St. Lawrence River	Fri	June 24	3:00 PM
Cruise 1000 Islands of the St. Lawrence				
Ar. Ogdensburg, N.Y.	St. Lawrence River	Fri	June 24	5:00 PM
Lv. OGDENSBURG, N.Y.	St. Lawrence River	Fri	June 24	6:00 PM
Iroquois Lock (6 feet)	Canadian			
Eisenhower Lock (51½ feet)	American			
Snell Lock (51½ feet)	American			
Beauharnois Locks—Upper, 41 ft.; Lower, 41 ft.				
St. Catherine Lock (35 feet)	Canadian			
St. Lambert Lock (15 feet)	Canadian			
Ar. Montreal, Quebec	St. Lawrence River	Sat	June 25	3:00 PM
Lv. MONTREAL, QUEBEC	St. Lawrence River	Sun	June 26	12:00 NOON
Ar. Ogdensburg, N.Y.	St. Lawrence River	Mon	June 27	9:30 AM
Lv. Ogdensburg, N.Y.	St. Lawrence River	Mon	June 27	11:00 AM
Pass Alexandria Bay, N.Y.	St. Lawrence River			
Pass Thousand Island Bridge	St. Lawrence River			
Pass Clayton, New York	St. Lawrence River	Mon	June 27	3:00 PM
Pass Cape Vincent, New York	St. Lawrence River	Mon	June 27	6:00 PM
Enter Welland Canal	Port Weller, Ont.	Tues	June 28	8:00 AM
Leave Welland Canal	Port Colborne, Ont.	Wed	June 29	2:00 AM
Ar. Buffalo, N.Y.	Lake Erie	Wed	June 29	5:00 AM
(Buffalo passengers disembark)				
Lv. Buffalo, N.Y.	Lake Erie	Wed	June 29	7:30 AM
Ar. Cleveland, Ohio	Lake Erie	Wed	June 29	7:45 PM
Lv. Cleveland, Ohio	Lake Erie	Wed	June 29	11:59 PM
Ar. Detroit, Mich.	Detroit River	Thur	June 30	8:00 AM
Lv. Detroit, Mich.	Detroit River	Thur	June 30	11:00 AM
Ar. Mackinac Island	Sts. of Mackinac	Fri	July 1	9:00 AM
Lv. Mackinac Island	Sts. of Mackinac	Fri	July 1	11:45 AM
Ar. Chicago, Ill.	Lake Michigan	Sat	July 2	11:15 AM

Note: All times shown west of Cleveland are Eastern Standard Time. All times east of Cleveland are Eastern Daylight Saving Time.

ROUND-TRIP RATES—PER PERSON

	DECK "C"	DECK "B"	DECK "A"	BEDROOMS
From—Chicago	$310.00	$345.00	$360.00	$610.00
Detroit	230.00	255.00	270.00	410.00
Cleveland	220.00	245.00	260.00	400.00
Buffalo	210.00	235.00	250.00	390.00
*Ogdensburg	135.00	160.00	175.00	305.00

Rates shown above are per person basis two to a room. Meals, transportation, sleeping accommodations, entertainment and Federal Tax on transportation and sleeping accommodations are included. Seaway Lock Tolls on all Roundtrip tickets, $15.00 extra.

*Plus $7.50 Seaway Tolls on Ogdensburg Roundtrip Tickets.

RATES—ONE WAY—TO OR FROM MONTREAL

Chicago	195.00	213.00	222.00	365.00
Detroit	127.50	142.50	152.50	230.00
Cleveland	122.50	137.50	147.50	225.00
Buffalo	117.50	132.50	142.50	220.00

Plus $7.50 Seaway Tolls on all One-Way Tickets.

Back Cover

BE ABOARD ONE OF THESE

TOP CRUISES OF THE YEAR

From GREAT LAKES PORTS all the way to MONTREAL and return!

Here's an opportunity to see the great, new St. Lawrence Seaway and cruise the Great Lakes, too . . . an opportunity to view America's New Fourth Coastline in its entirety. It's the cruise of the year . . . a vacation you will cherish in rich memories for years to come.

Think of it! From Chicago all the way to Montreal and return. Rest, relaxation, fun, frolic, scenic beauty, visits to delightful resort areas and exciting port cities . . . there'll never be a dull moment as your ship cruises enchanting waterways, visits historical areas and provides you with all of the comforts and conveniences of home.

And, of course, one of the highlights of your trip will be the passage of your ship through the great locks and the man-made waterways of the magnificent, new St. Lawrence Seaway. You'll get a broader understanding of the meaning of this breath-taking development as your ship is lowered and raised hundreds of feet in the massive locks and as you view ships from many nations, the world over, carrying products to and from mid-western world ports.

Read inside where you'll go . . . what you'll do . . . and other things you will see. Then make your reservations early . . . for these cruises will be sell-outs. They are the only round-trip cruises to the Seaway this year.

THERE WILL BE NO ROUND-TRIP SEAWAY CRUISES DURING JULY AND AUGUST.

CHICAGO . . . the Commercial Capital of Mid-America

You'll visit world-famous Mackinac Island

DETROIT . . . the World's Automobile Capital

Through the great locks of the new Seaway

Visit MONTREAL . . . the metropolis of Canada

B. Brochure (W4IWH Collection)

Cover

Your stop at Mackinac Island allows plenty of time to explore this Island of History.

Through the "Soo" Locks . . . you'll surely want to be on deck for this.

your cruise of America's Great Inland Seas is a cruise of the world's most interesting waterways

No cruising area in the world more richly combines the beauty, historic interest and diversity of attractions as the Great Lakes Region. And more so now than ever before! For the opening of the great, new St. Lawrence Seaway has brought ships from many lands into these waters. You'll see ships from ports the world over. You'll see flags of many nations. You'll marvel at the work being done to change our Great Lakes port cities into world ports. And you will appreciate the meaning of what "America's New Fourth Coastline" means to America's future economy. From the sky-blue waters and verdant forests of the North to the great industrial centers of the southern lakes, this region of more than 94,000 square miles of water area is a cruising delight. The Great Lakes are truly America's Water Wonderland. A cruise of these waters belongs in your experience.

Sun, fun, music, blue skies, blue waters! They are all part of your Great Lakes cruise.

Rest and relax as a continuous panorama of scenic beauty unfolds before your eyes.

Scenic waterways, interesting ports-of-call – be sure to bring your camera and plenty of film.

sail away for a truly Thrilling Vacation

YOU'LL FIND EVERY FACILITY FOR YOUR COMFORT, CONVENIENCE AND PLEASURE

aboard the

S.S. NORTH AMERICAN • S.S. SOUTH AMERICAN

Come to the Captain's Dinner! It's a gala event. Fun, music . . . and food that's a gourmet's delight.

Which is your vacation preference? Rest? Relaxation? Gay parties? Dancing? Sight seeing? Whatever your choice you'll find it aboard your Great Lakes cruise ship. Combine them all if you wish. *Afloat* there will be carefree days of deck games, strolling, sun bathing or just lazing in your favorite deck chair. There will be evenings of entertainment, dancing, gay parties. You'll spend pleasant hours in the Binnacle Bar. And at night you will enjoy the priceless boon of untroubled sleep. *Ashore* there'll be fascinating visits to the most scenic, historic and interesting ports of the Great Lakes region, where there will be plenty of time for sightseeing and shopping. And with all this, the superb cuisine and the gracious service for which the Georgian Bay Line has become justly famous. Here is a vacation you will live over and over again in pleasant and exciting memories.

Like to dance? Then swing away under the stars in the ship's ballroom each evening.

Have a cocktail? Then meet your friends in the Binnacle Bar for a pre-dinner drink.

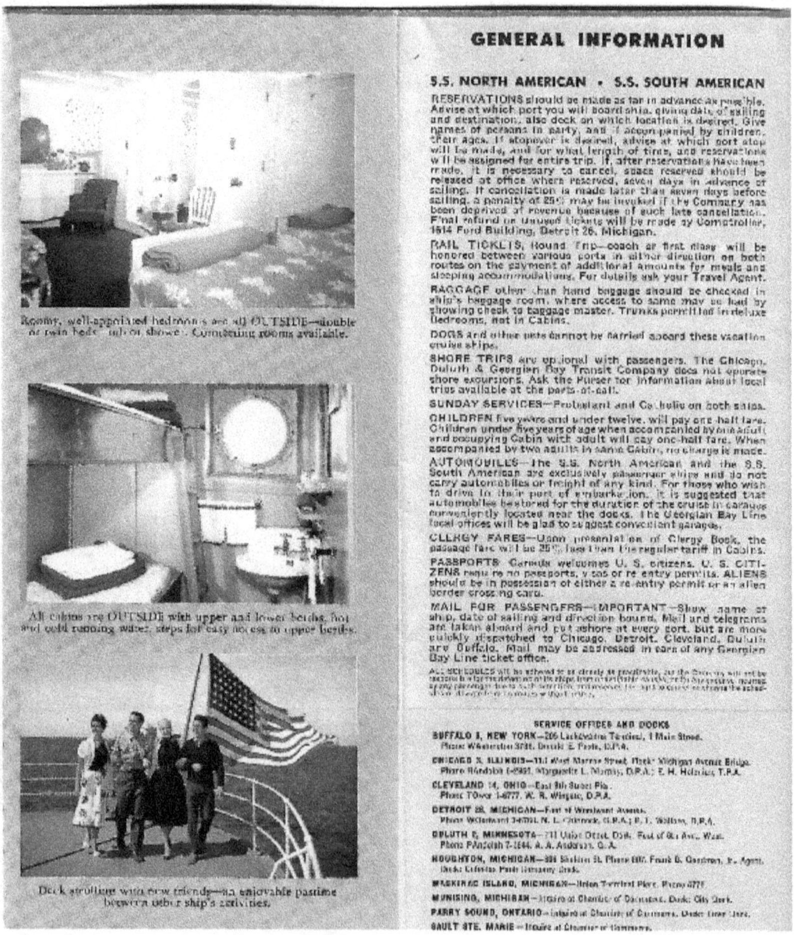

Roomy, well-appointed bedrooms are all OUTSIDE—double or twin beds—tub or shower. Connecting rooms available.

All cabins are OUTSIDE with upper and lower berths, hot and cold running water; steps for easy access to upper berths.

Deck strolling with new friends—an enjoyable pastime between other ship's activities.

GENERAL INFORMATION

S.S. NORTH AMERICAN • S.S. SOUTH AMERICAN

RESERVATIONS should be made as far in advance as possible. Advise at which port you will board ship, giving date of sailing and destination, also deck on which location is desired. Give names of persons in party, and if accompanied by children, their ages. If stopover is desired, advise at which port stop will be made, and for what length of time, and reservations will be assigned for entire trip. If, after reservations have been made, it is necessary to cancel, space reserved should be released at office where reserved, seven days in advance of sailing. If cancellation is made later than seven days before sailing, a penalty of 25% may be invoked if the Company has been deprived of revenue because of such late cancellation. Final refund on unused tickets will be made by Comptroller, 1614 Ford Building, Detroit 26, Michigan.

RAIL TICKETS, Round Trip—coach or first class will be honored between various ports in either direction on both routes on the payment of additional amounts for meals and sleeping accommodations. For details ask your Travel Agent.

BAGGAGE other than hand baggage should be checked in ship's baggage room, where access to same may be had by showing check to baggage master. Trunks permitted in deluxe Bedrooms, not in Cabins.

DOGS and other pets cannot be carried aboard these vacation cruise ships.

SHORE TRIPS are optional with passengers. The Chicago, Duluth & Georgian Bay Transit Company does not operate shore excursions. Ask the Purser for information about local trips available at the ports-of-call.

SUNDAY SERVICES—Protestant and Catholic on both ships.

CHILDREN five years and under twelve, will pay one-half fare. Children under five years of age when accompanied by one adult and occupying Cabin with adult will pay one-half fare. When accompanied by two adults in same Cabin, no charge is made.

AUTOMOBILES—The S.S. North American and the S.S. South American are exclusively passenger ships and do not carry automobiles or freight of any kind. For those who wish to drive to their port of embarkation, it is suggested that automobiles be stored for the duration of the cruise in garages conveniently located near the docks. The Georgian Bay Line local offices will be glad to suggest convenient garages.

CLERGY FARES—Upon presentation of Clergy Book, the passage fare will be 25% less than the regular tariff in Cabins.

PASSPORTS Canada welcomes U. S. citizens. U. S. CITIZENS require no passports, visas or re-entry permits. ALIENS should be in possession of either a re-entry permit or an alien border crossing card.

MAIL FOR PASSENGERS—IMPORTANT—Show name of ship, date of sailing and direction bound. Mail and telegrams are taken aboard and put ashore at every port, but are more quickly dispatched to Chicago, Detroit, Cleveland, Duluth and Buffalo. Mail may be addressed in care of any Georgian Bay Line ticket office.

ALL SCHEDULES will be adhered to as closely as practicable, but the Company will not be [illegible]

SERVICE OFFICES AND DOCKS

BUFFALO 3, NEW YORK—205 Lackawanna Terminal, 1 Main Street. Phone: WAshington [illegible]. [illegible], D.P.A.

CHICAGO 3, ILLINOIS—[illegible] West Monroe Street. Dock: Michigan Avenue Bridge. Phone RAndolph [illegible]. [illegible], D.P.A.; E. H. [illegible], T.P.A.

CLEVELAND 14, OHIO—East 9th Street Pier. Phone TOwer 1-6777. W. R. [illegible], D.P.A.

DETROIT 26, MICHIGAN—Foot of Woodward Avenue. Phone WOodward [illegible]. N. L. [illegible], G.P.A.; [illegible], D.P.A.

DULUTH 2, MINNESOTA—[illegible]. Dock: Foot of [illegible] Ave., West. Phone RAndolph 7-[illegible]. A. A. Anderson, G. A.

HOUGHTON, MICHIGAN—[illegible] Shelden St. Phone [illegible]. Frank B. [illegible], Jr., Agent. Dock: [illegible].

MACKINAC ISLAND, MICHIGAN—Union Terminal Pier. Phone [illegible].

MUNISING, MICHIGAN—Inquire at Chamber of Commerce. Dock: City Dock.

PARRY SOUND, ONTARIO—Inquire at Chamber of Commerce. Dock: [illegible].

SAULT STE. MARIE—Inquire at Chamber of Commerce.

C. Cabin Layout (W4IWH Collection)

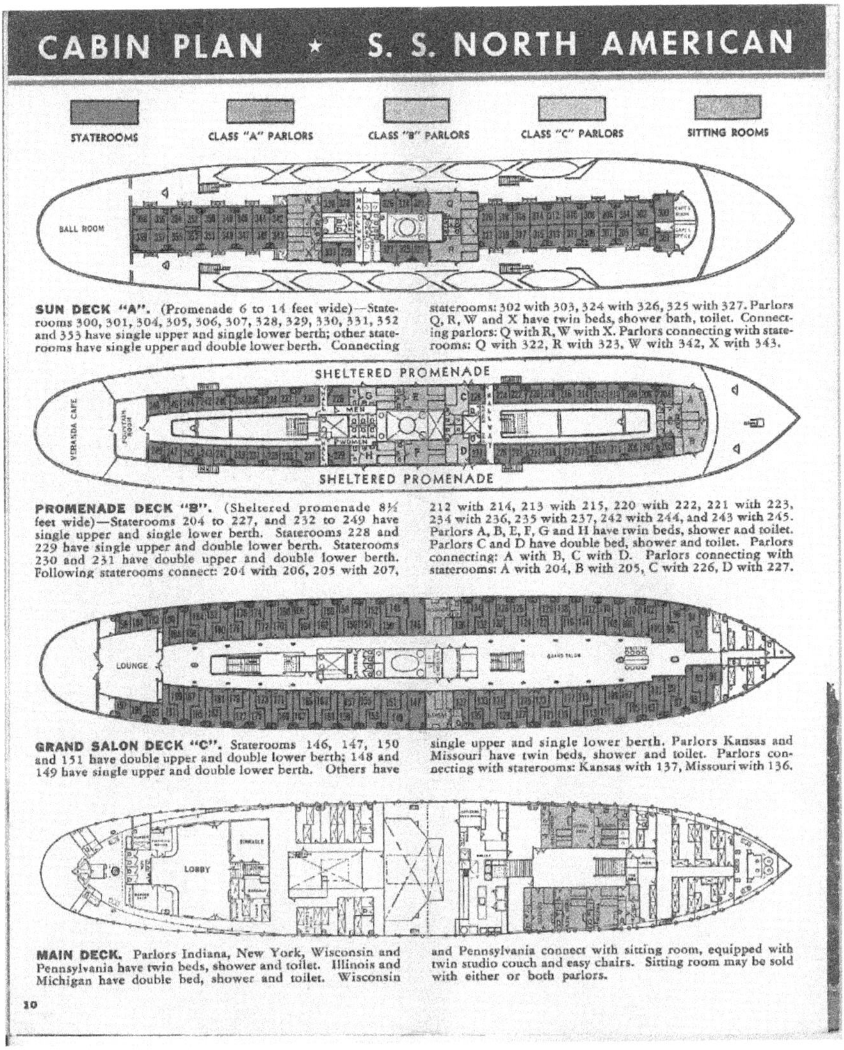

CABIN PLAN ★ S. S. NORTH AMERICAN

SUN DECK "A". (Promenade 6 to 14 feet wide)—Staterooms 300, 301, 304, 305, 306, 307, 328, 329, 330, 331, 352 and 353 have single upper and single lower berth; other staterooms have single upper and double lower berth. Connecting staterooms: 302 with 303, 324 with 326, 325 with 327. Parlors Q, R, W and X have twin beds, shower bath, toilet. Connecting parlors: Q with R, W with X. Parlors connecting with staterooms: Q with 322, R with 323, W with 342, X with 343.

PROMENADE DECK "B". (Sheltered promenade 8½ feet wide)—Staterooms 204 to 227, and 232 to 249 have single upper and single lower berth. Staterooms 228 and 229 have single upper and double lower berth. Staterooms 230 and 231 have double upper and double lower berth. Following staterooms connect: 204 with 206, 205 with 207, 212 with 214, 213 with 215, 220 with 222, 221 with 223, 234 with 236, 235 with 237, 242 with 244, and 243 with 245. Parlors A, B, E, F, G and H have twin beds, shower and toilet. Parlors C and D have double bed, shower and toilet. Parlors connecting: A with B, C with D. Parlors connecting with staterooms: A with 204, B with 205, C with 226, D with 227.

GRAND SALON DECK "C". Staterooms 146, 147, 150 and 151 have double upper and double lower berth; 148 and 149 have single upper and double lower berth. Others have single upper and single lower berth. Parlors Kansas and Missouri have twin beds, shower and toilet. Parlors connecting with staterooms: Kansas with 137, Missouri with 136.

MAIN DECK. Parlors Indiana, New York, Wisconsin and Pennsylvania have twin beds, shower and toilet. Illinois and Michigan have double bed, shower and toilet. Wisconsin and Pennsylvania connect with sitting room, equipped with twin studio couch and easy chairs. Sitting room may be sold with either or both parlors.

10

D. Menu

S.S. North American
S.S. South American

The Captain's Dinner has a long, distinguished tradition behind it dating way back to the old sailing days. No one knew then precisely when the ship would make port because of rough weather and uncertain navigational patterns. When land was finally sighted, and it was certain that the ship would arrive safely in the port the next day, they had a gala celebration with all the remaining food on board served up the night before disembarking. However, no food was eaten until prayers were offered to God for his safe guidance during the voyage.

☆

Executive Staff

S. S. NORTH AMERICAN

CAPTAIN RUSSELL A. PICARD
Master

THEODORE WEBSTER
Chief Purser

ROY F. MONROE
Chief Engineer

WALTER J. COLLEY
Chief Steward

CHICAGO, DULUTH AND GEORGIAN BAY TRANSIT CO.

S. S. NORTH AMERICAN

Captain's Dinner

☆ ☆

ICED CELERY — QUEEN AND RIPE OLIVES — ROSE RADISHES

SPICED FRUIT — CHILLED TOMATO JUICE
SMOKED SALMON — FRESH SHRIMP COCKTAIL

FRENCH ONION SOUP WITH CROUTONS

SAUTE GREAT LAKES TROUT, LEMON WEDGE
MAINE LOBSTER A LA NEWBURG IN PATTY SHELL
ROAST PRIME RIBS OF BEEF, AU JUS

FRESH GREEN PEAS — WHOLE BABY BEETS
OVEN BROWN OR DELMONICO POTATOES

CHEF'S SALAD WITH SPECIAL DRESSING

HOT DINNER ROLLS — ASSORTED BREADS AND CRACKERS

FRENCH APPLE PIE — ORANGE LAYER CAKE
FRESH FRUIT (IN SEASON) — FROZEN RASPBERRY SUNDAE
VANILLA OR BUTTER PECAN ICE CREAM
AND COOKIES
CHEDDAR, ROQUEFORT OR CAMEMBERT CHEESE

COFFEE — TEA — MILK — BUTTERMILK
ICED TEA — ICED COFFEE — SANKA

1000 7-60 — CD-N

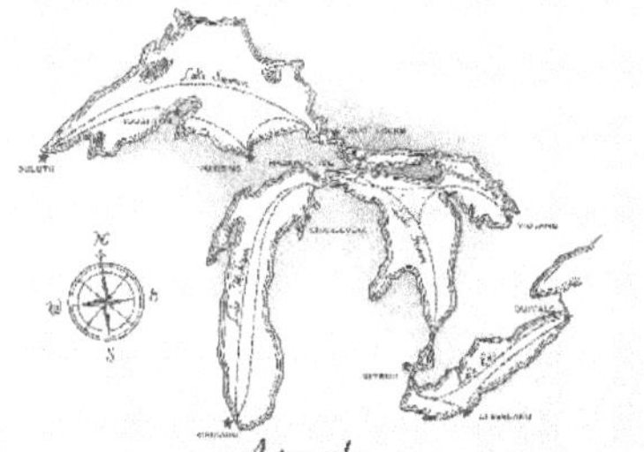

Autographs

E. Diary

The following is a diary I kept during the summer of 1960 while I was the Third Radio Operator aboard the *SS North American.* The first and last pages of the diary are water logged so it is sketchy but the other pages are in good shape. The diary is a little cryptic during early June but picks up when we ran aground on June 24.

Approximately June 2: I took a train and met ? Ate breakfast and drove to Grosse Pointe and Detroit. Grosse Pointe is a beautiful old town. I saw the North American in the Detroit River and it was bigger than I expected. I went to the Ford Building and met Miss Olsen in ?? I took a cab to the ship in the pouring rain. I met John Flynn, the 3rd Mate and Henry Waite and took a tour of the ship. I sacked out until 4 PM and then took my first watch from 4 to 8 PM. After this, I stood in the very bow of the ship and watched the lights of Cleveland as we approached. The weather was clear.

June 3: Saw Niagara Falls for the first time. Very impressive!

June 4: We traveled up the St. Lawrence River through the Thousand Islands area. Very beautiful with old castles and homes perched on tiny islands.

June 5: Arrived in Montreal, took a sightseeing bus and discovered our driver was French Canadian. He spoke only broken English and was very corny but kept us in stitches. Montreal is an amazing city. It has small French pastry shops, a mountain that overlooks the city and a huge cathedral. It has all hand carved wood interior. After the trip, Mel, Andrea, Lorain and I walked back to town to the Hotel Berkely, a sidewalk café, but it was closing. We took off on our own and found a whole string of French pastry and coffee houses. We ended up at Pam Pam's and talked a blond waitress into giving us some menus. Soon the manager was over to see us and we got a grand tour of the place. Very friendly people! We met some kids off the boat and promised a rendezvous at the House of Rock & Roll. On the way I asked a cop how to get there and with the language barrier and all we both ended up just shaking our heads and laughing.

June 7: Met a waitress named Joyce and she talked me into joining the Crew Show. I signed on as a member of the Crew Show singing a group Thanksgiving number, "Let All Things Now Living".

June 8: We arrived in Toronto and took a sightseeing trip. They have nothing but Toronto University and a new subway.

June 13: John and Henry left, Phil and Ben aboard. Weather is very rough so we anchored inside the breakwater for the Purple Heart Cruise. We never left the pier for the dinner dance cruise. Deadhead (a passage with only the crew on board) was rough but most made it ok.

June 14 to 16: Grand Rapids Chamber of Commerce. Weather rainy and foggy. The group was drunk the whole trip and I chased some guy, who didn't even know where he was, out of the Harem (a term we used to describe a place where the waitresses lived.) I met Bob Schultz at Milwaukee.

June 16 to 17: Holland, Michigan to Chicago deadhead. Weather was very rough. We were in the trough of the waves and I measured a 20 to 35 degree roll. Phone books, fan, etc. flew off the shelves. I got seasick. UGH! (I remember this storm to this very day nearly 50 years later as one of the worst I have ever experienced. Winds were running 70 MPH and I think the anemometer broke so we really didn't know how windy it became. I spoke with the Mate in the pilothouse and he was concerned that the windows would blow in. I suspect we were in danger of rolling and sinking. This was one of only two times in my life that I have been seasick.)

June 18: Cloudy with winds South at 18 knots, scattered showers. We docked at Charlevoix, MI with the High School band marching on the dock, banners flying and a crowd of people. Courtesy cars were made available to tour the town and there were signs in the stores saying "Welcome SS North American!" Apparently, this was a big event for them.

We left at 3:30 PM for Mackinac Island with heavy overcast. We made the Mackinac Bridge at 1930 and docked in Mackinac at 2008 with skies cloudy but the threat of rain gone. Joyce and I walked around to the right of the pier to see the natural bridge. We walked for half an hour and were about ready to give up when we saw some rustic steps up the side of a heavily wooded shear cliff. We decided to explore so we climbed about 200 or 300 feet through a washed out old trail and finally came to some shelters and a cement runway. This runway lead out to the natural bridge that we originally had set out to see. We stayed there and watched ships sail past, etc. until 2205 (The ship sails at 2300). We started down the path but soon became lost. At one point I was moving down the path and my left leg fell through a hole in the path and I dropped to my right knee and caught myself. By climbing up and down the cliff and backtracking whenever we were lost, we made it down the cliff at 2225. We ran part of the way back to the ship but made it at 2242.

We left Mackinac Island at 2310. At 0002 weather via radio station WMI said winds S-SW at 12 and the weather is fine, few showers extreme south tonight. Notwithstanding the "fine" weather report, I saw a lightning storm in the distance and had to ground the antennas occasionally. (The radio "shack" was on top of the ship and the antenna was a long wire stretching the length of the ship from masts. On the roof of the shack, the wire came in and went through a knife switch. The knife could go in two directions: to the radio or to the metal hull. In the later position, the antennas were "grounded" to the hull and into the water so that the antenna appeared, to lightning, no higher than the water. We used to have fun in lightning storms by slightly removing the knife switch from the ground position to see how large a spark we could draw. That was not very smart but then again we were 20-year-old kids!)

Destination: Milwaukee via Green Bay, Sturgeon Bay and the ship canal.

June 19, 0010 to 0145: I listened to a distress call from the Dutch motor vessel, Gertie Buisnks that ran aground south of White Shoal Light. She was in no immediate danger and the Coast Guard was coming at dawn to pull her off.

1030 EST woke up and saw entrance to Sturgeon Bay. The sun was out and it looked very pretty. I saw the ship yards and Baudhoin Yacht Harbor, which hadn't changed much since I saw it a couple of years ago while cruising on my parents boat. We passed through the ship canal and saw all the people sitting on the bank fishing.

1209 LAFOT (Short for Lakes Forecast, I think) weather via radio station WAY: 1. Fine NE-N @13 diminishing 2. Fine E 10 becoming fine SE-S @12

1230: On Lake Michigan bound for Milwaukee

1330: Some 15 year old kids are flying a kite from the Tea Room. (A deck on the stern of the boat with a little café). It looks like it's out half a mile!

2030: I did my number in the crew show and it went ok. Joyce and Wayne did an encore. (Joyce and Wayne had opera-trained voices and did several solos and duets in the show). The hit of the show is a square dance number with boys using mops as partners!

2130: We docked a half hour early at Milwaukee. I saw the Military Art Center. It was a very modern building with meeting rooms and "strange" paintings all over.

2300: We left for Chicago. Phil (my cousin and 1st Radio Operator) drove Goebel's car from Milwaukee to Chicago so Ben (the 2nd Radio Officer) took the 12 to 6 shift and I will work 6 to 4 tomorrow. (Goebel was the Executive Vice President of the Georgian Bay Lines)

June 20, 0609: WAY LAFOT weather: 1. Mostly clear, SE @10 becoming SE @15. 2. Cloudy SE-S @18 chance of thunder showers

0614: Docked in Chicago

0645: Called home. Parents had a good trip to Kenosha on their boat

0650: Changing channel 30 to 38 for seaway trip #2. (Back then, radios operated on fixed frequencies and you had to change the crystal to different channels. Also, the equipment used tubes and hence was large and heavy. Our transmitter was in a rack of equipment about 6 feet high and 18 inches wide.)

0900: Bob Martin and Dad came down to the ship. Joyce showed Bob around.

1100: We sailed for Mackinac Island, our first stop on our second Seaway cruise

2100: I listened to the Patterson-Johansson fight. Patterson clobbered him cold in the 5th--great fight. I played a card game called "Down the River" which is very exciting and fun!

June 21, 0002: WMI LAFOT weather. 1. Mostly clear ESE @ 13N; cloudy E @ 15 2. Cloudy ESE 17N; cloudy ESE 20

0930: Docked at Mackinac Island and had fire and lifeboat drill. My hose is on the starboard side of the radio shack. The wind was blowing fairly hard and the people on "B" deck were soaked! Our lifeboat was first down and up again as usual. I lucked out because our lifeboat is the only one that has an electric drill that is converted to a portable winch motor. The other boats have to be cranked up by hand, which is quite a job. The weather was crystal clear and the island was beautiful. Now we are bound for Detroit and should pass the South American on Lake Huron this afternoon.

1200 LAFOT weather via WMI Huron: 1. Cloudy E-SE @12 2. Cloudy SE 18 followed by rain

1500: I got a big shock when I touched the bug and the CW receiver. (The "bug" was a device used to send Morse Code or "CW"). There was 110 volts DC between these and I was lucky the weather was dry because I jumped right off. Lake Huron is completely calm except for a few wind ripples. The temperature has been very cold for the last two weeks. Where's summer??

1545: We passed the South American with much whistle blowing and waving and shouting!

June 22, 0002: WMI LAFOT Huron: 1 and 2. Cloudy E-SE @13.

1000: We docked in Detroit in the rain as usual. Joyce and I walked up town and bought some supplies. When we got back, we learned her grandfather died. She's quite upset.

1209: LAFOT WAY Erie: Small craft warnings up noon EST Wednesday. 1. Thunder squalls, S-SE @17, winds briefly 30 knots, scattered thundershowers 2. Shifting winds becoming showers NW @15.

2100: We docked in Cleveland. Weather is hazy but warming up.

2200: We left Cleveland bound for Thorold, Ontario.

June 23, 0009 EST: WAY LAFOT weather: Small craft warnings down 11:30 PM EST. 1 & 2: Cloudy variable @13; a few showers and fog

1124: Had considerable fog in early morning (about 5 or 6) and the foghorn kept waking me up. (The foghorn was on the ship's smokestack right above the radio shack).

We tied up at Lock #8 on the Welland canal for over an hour so it looks like we will be late into Thorold, Ontario. This will probably mean no Niagara Falls trip for the passengers. We are leaving Lock #8 now and should proceed without too much delay to Thorold. The weather is quite warm and humid. The skies are a little hazy and cloudy but it is nice and sunny.

1202: LAFOT WMI Ontario: 1. Cloudy E-SE @13 increasing to showers E-SE @22. 2. Thundersqualls E-SE @24.

Afternoon: We entered the Welland Ship Canal. The weather was foggy and so pictures might not turn out too good.

1340: We docked at Thorold, Ontario. We hitched a ride in the back of a pickup truck and Joyce and I went bowling. My hook is still giving me a little trouble but is coming around.

2100: We had an impromptu songfest on the fantail where the crew hangs out.

June 24: LAFOT WAY Ontario. Small Craft Warnings in effect. 1. Cloudy S-SW @15 briefly higher in thunderstorms. 2. Showers S-SW@25 becoming showers W-NW 30 and diminishing.

0300: Phil overslept and I had to go in and rack him out.

1100: Ben forgot to wake me up until 1200. Must be good for sleeping last night! Weather is rainy, which is too bad because we are now cruising the St. Lawrence River. Many passengers are mad at the weather and are cancelling the rest of the trip.

1400: The sun is peeking out as we pass through the Thousand Islands area. We have a strong tail wind of 34 MPH. The river is very rough.

1600: We arrived at Ogdensburg Harbor and promptly ran aground. (Here, the diary has a map showing the channel and how we ran aground). The ship was apparently very difficult to control in the high winds and in trying to avoid being blown ashore, we overcorrected for the wind and ran up on a clay bar in the middle of the river. We tried for ¾ of an hour to pull ourselves free but no luck. Passengers are calm and there is no apparent danger.

2100: A big tug came from across the river and tried for half an hour to pull us free but had no luck. We didn't budge an inch. VBX21 says that they won't let us in the seaway anyways because of gale force winds so here we sit. The log reads "1100: On watch sunk at Ogdensburg"

The Crew Show went on as usual tonight. I am now in three numbers. "Look Ahead", the opening, which is a group song and dance; "Let All Things Now Living", a serious group song that we close with; and a duet with Ralph Church, the Third Purser, on "16 Tons". Tonight was our first try at the duet and it was sick! Our voices don't match, his being a tenor and mine a bass. He has a sick hillbilly style and clutches badly. This plus my own inexperience screwed us up.

We are still stuck in the shallows! We are drawing quite a crowd on the shore and the local radio station has been interrupting their program material with somewhat distorted "bulletins". This is all very amusing especially since the Executive Vice President, Mr. Goebel, was waiting ashore ready to come aboard for the seaway cruise. Also we have an experienced St. Lawrence Seaway Pilot aboard whom we are paying to guide us safely through the Seaway. The rumor is that we will take busses to Montreal in the morning.

June 25, 0000: Mr. Goebel and Mr. Turnbull came in and set up an emergency walkie-talkie to the Ogdensburg Police Department. I will call every half hour and check for messages.

1100: We are stuck!!!! The tug America and the tug Robinson Bay have been pulling since 0530 this morning and we haven't budged. Mr. Gobel is surprisingly calm through this whole mess.

1400: The tugs are still pulling but no luck. Our water supply is gone and the toilets are clogged or backing up or flushing continuously. This could be a bad situation. A ferry came over to take passengers to Prescott where they will board the train for Montreal. Only 62 took the trip though as most of the passengers are staying with the feeble hope of seeing the locks. If we are off by evening, we'll still make the trip. Morale is still quite high and as the weather is sunny and clear, no one is too unhappy.

1100: The ferry came with a water truck to use for washing dishes. It disappeared quickly and we were able to fill a few glasses for future use. The radio shack has been swamped with hotel cancellations and messages as well as tug traffic, etc. During and after lunch, the public address system was in almost constant use.

The ferry came again at 1630 EDST and took passengers to Ogdensburg, the return trip being at 1900 EDST. No crewmember is allowed ashore. Another tug, Miss Lana, arrived and began to help the other two. This afternoon one tug rocked the bow while the other pulled the stern. We moved a few inches but they abandoned this procedure for some reason. The three tugs gave up at 2300 EST tonight after accomplishing nothing. We are in a mess with no water or proper facilities. They might have to dredge us out and then dry-dock us. Mr. Collie, Chief Steward, told the waitresses that they might be fired for a week or so until the hull can be repaired. The local people are having a ball circling the ship in their speedboats and lining the banks. The local newspaper gave us headlines and three big photos on the front page.

The morale is somewhat down. The crew is frantic to get ashore and the passengers are very upset about missing connections with friends. One couple was unable to stop their two sons from flying to Montreal from Chicago to meet them. We are so close to the shore (100 yards) and yet are unable to get there!

June 26, 0110: A tug is coming out with provisions.

1100: We now have five tugs ready to pull. Two are on a line to our stern and three are forward on the port side. Also, two dredges are coming to help us if the tugs can't do it.

The sun is very hot and people are just roasting and sweating. Since there is no water to wash with, the whole ship stinks!

Evening: The tugs pulled all afternoon without moving us an inch. Just before we ran aground, the skipper radioed Iroquois Lock that our draft was 15 feet, 6 inches. A check this afternoon revealed that we are at about 10 feet, which means we are 5 feet away from floating! We are really high and dry! About dinner time a seagoing tug, Melanie Fair, from London arrived and will help pull in the morning. It is a monster and is supposed to have over 2000 HP but the general consensus of the engineers is that it will have little effect.

So far, the following tugs and their HP are involved:

Salvage Monarch—1400 HP

Salvage Prince—500 HP

Robinson Bay—1400 HP

America—1000 HP

Miss Lana—1250 HP

In addition, the Monarch and Prince have special anchors that they secure in the mud and then use big bow winches to get extra pull.

Tomorrow, the passengers can take a bus tour to the Eisenhower and Snell Locks. Many people took the trip just to see these locks so they should be happier. If the tugs can't do anything tomorrow, they'll send the passengers home and start dredging. This will take 3 to 5 days.

We got some water tonight and both Ben and I crowded into our small room and took dry showers. I really feel good now for the first time in a couple of days. We have been hoarding drinking water in two glasses and a paper cup, and we found we could wash our hands by turning on an auxiliary fire hose socket at my fire station on the side of the radio shack. Passenger morale is still ok but crew is very poor. They need some time ashore very badly!

June 27, 0034: LAFOT weather Ontario: 1. Fine S-SW @15 2. Fine SW @15 Occasional cloudy SW @ 20. The Eisenhower Lock sent a Security Call saying that the SS Invar was aground below the Snell Lock so apparently we weren't the only ones to run into difficulties.

1135: The new tug from London was working with the others but no luck. They are eating lunch now and plotting! If we are not off by tonight, most of the crew will be sent home according to Beauregard and Collie. I just called WBL using Morse Code and had IBIY, an Italian ship, call me back. He was either a poor sender or half of his stuff was sent in Italian. He wanted me to relay a message free of charge and when I asked where to, he said "Roma Radio Italy". We went back and forth confusing each other more and more and he finally sent "OK, never mind!" Whew!

June 28: 0050 to0230: The tugs tried their all yesterday but we didn't budge. Capt. Piccard is really dragging. They are going to send the passengers home tomorrow morning and the crew shortly thereafter. Tomorrow, dredging will begin and after that they will work on the ship in dry dock for a while. I still don't know whether I'm going or staying. This will just about bankrupt the Georgian Bay Lines and there is serious doubt whether or not they will operate next year.

Tonight, Don Kirby, an 18 year old from the Ogdensburg Journal came aboard and I spent a good deal of time talking to him and showing him around the ship so maybe my name will be in print tomorrow! Their paper is really lousy and they are really having a ball trying to place the blame on someone. I've been working my tail off for 3-1/2 hours sending messages and arranging for buses with the police. I'm exhausted and so is everyone else. We have been minus water all day but got some tonight. I never knew how good it could feel to wash my face!

We have had all sorts of strange folk in the shack. The Britishers off the Melanie Fair are very smart and proper and their accent is very interesting. The man in charge is Scottish so this is rapidly becoming and international affair.

The passengers left this morning. Most crew are only working about half their hours now so there is an almost festive air aboard the boat. It's like the feeling you have when finals are over and you're about ready to go home. No one really knows what is going to be done with the crew yet but we are all expecting an announcement this afternoon. The weather is still sunny and nice and morale is quite high.

June 29, 0017: The Steward's Department, Pursers and all were laid off this afternoon. Only about 17 will remain. The dredges started work this afternoon and it looks like a long tedious process. They will work around the clock to free us. Tonight, the crew got shore leave for the first time since June 23. Most went wild and got drunk at Oscar's. Joyce and I took the ferry to Prescott and saw an old fort, etc. I took a shower for the first time in many days.

1130: We are getting the first cloudy weather we've had for many days and it should rain for a while. They've dug a ditch along the port side of the ship and now they are going to bury a Deadman ashore and use winches on this. (A Deadman is a pit full of concrete and lumber to create an anchor on shore). Also, they will use a bulldozer pulling a cable to try and get us off this thing. The weather may hamper things though. Most of the crew left this morning and the ship is dead.

June 30: 0040: They buried some concrete and junk in a hole ashore and connected the Prince between it and the ship. Miss Lana pushed our starboard and Melanie Fair held the bow in case we came free. When the signal to go came the ship tilted a little, the Deadman was torn up and we broke a bit in the bow! We're still stuck!! Today, they will build a stronger Deadman and try again. The Englishmen are charming and some of the waitresses who are still hanging around are carrying on big affairs.

1150: (The diary has a map here that shows trenches in the shape of a tic-tac-toe grid on shore filled with lumber and a cable connecting the Deadman through a tug to the ship.)

At present, they are still working on it. I'm hoping that we will be free this afternoon. I think we moved a little yesterday but the Deadman was torn up.

2300: We're free! About 1600 EDST the tugs started pulling again. I took a sighting on a bridge to our stern and at first, I couldn't tell whether we were actually moving or just listing but soon it was evident that the stern was swinging toward shore. It moved very slowly and at 1638 we became buoyant. The Melanie Fair, which held a line to our bow, took off immediately but the cable, which is as big as my wrist, snapped. There was a strong on-shore breeze and we started blowing ashore. We dropped our anchor and came out of any danger. Meanwhile the Melanie Fair was in reverse and had run over the broken cable. Luckily, it didn't snag in the prop for if it had, she would have blown ashore on the rocks. Finally, everyone got straightened out and we made it to the city dock on our own power. It was s strange but pleasant feeling to be under way again. The hull of the North is all dirty, scratched and dented but there is no apparent damage. Tomorrow the Coast Guard will inspect her and then we will sail for Buffalo where we will start our season Tuesday, July 5. Tonight, in celebration, I had one beer and then saw a show. There were two horrible outer space movies but they had films of the Patterson-Johansson fight that were real good.

July 1: 2300: Today was a beautiful sunny day. Some of the kids went water skiing but I was on duty. Tom, our busboy, and I had a drink and took in another show. This time they were a bit better but not too much. I played baseball for a while and it felt good to get some exercise. We sail at 12 noon tomorrow for Buffalo. Today the Coast Guard inspected us and we welded part of our bow back on where a chock had been ripped out. Also we scrubbed and repainted part of the hull. She looks as good as new!

July 2: 2300: Sailed for Buffalo at 1104 EST today amid much horn blowing and cheering and waving from the natives. Marty, the Social Director, handed out the usual streamers to the handful of maids and crew members who were on hand and Ben played some march music over the P.A. to take the place of our band. Capt. Picard took the flying bridge with a big grin on his face and then we left the thriving metropolis of Ogdensburg, NY. No one on board was too upset over leaving!! I'm afraid we upset the whole economy of the burg. The merchants won't know what to do with their increase in income due to the large expenditures made by the passengers and crew. Their paper sounded very sad at having us leave and rumor has it that the town is going to change the channel markers so that we will run aground next year!

We are now on Lake Ontario and should be at the Welland Canal between 2 AM and 4 AM tomorrow. We may have trouble going through because there is heavy traffic due to the fact that they stopped shipping at the Snell Lock for about 12 hours while they pulled the Inver out of the mud. The 6 PM LAFOT said 35 MPH winds and thunder squalls but it doesn't seem to be rough right now. The word must be out that we are under way again because we've had many small craft running circles around us. One card offered us his towline in case we "needed assistance"!!

July 3: 2330: We made it through the locks in record time and arrived at Port Colborne at 1300 EST. We can't dock at Buffalo until 6 tomorrow so we are sitting at a coal dock here. We can't get cleared through customs so no one can get off. The skipper must be scared of the ship or something for we had a bad time coming through the locks. We hit the port side very hard this morning and split the partition between rooms 106 and 108. Some of the striping around the windows was loose and there were splinters all over the floor. The starboard side was worse. We scraped up against the lock walls several times and scraped and gouged the wood strips on the hull on "B" Deck. Also, we broke two embarkation lights and smashed an air vent on the side. Also, there was a rumor of some portholes being broken but I didn't see them.

We had thunder squalls this afternoon but it cleared about 5 PM and it is now a beautiful clear night. I got hold of W2PPL on the sideband rig and he called Dick Holmes, a fraternity brother, but no one was home. (In those days, the mode of transmission was AM like your AM radio. However, a more efficient transmission mode called single sideband was being tested and we pioneered the use of "SSB" on the Great Lakes. The radio could also be used on the "ham" bands.) I tried later for an hour but couldn't contact a Buffalo station.

July 4, 2350: Phil took off for Niagara today with Pattie Peterson so I worked all afternoon. We are sitting at Buffalo. I've called Dick Holmes all day but I guess he's gone to the lakes. Tonight, we saw "Can, Can". It was pretty good and there were a lot of laughs. Afterwards, we went to Leonardo's but it was closed. We then went to Dan Montgomery's on Exchange St. I tried an old fashioned and a run and coke both of which were ok but I still like a Tom Collins best. Tomorrow we have an FCC inspection and a Fire and Lifeboat Drill and then at 7 PM EST we sail and are back on schedule.

July 5, 2330: This morning I awoke to the sound of the fire alarm about 11 AM. After recovering from the shock of hitting my head on the ceiling of our "hole", Phil entered announcing a Fire and Lifeboat Drill. I scrambled out the door about half dressed with my life preserver flying and went to my station. Today was a Federal inspection and since the other two fellows at my station were in the Stewards Department and hadn't showed up yet, I had to scramble. I started to lay out the hose but looked down and saw an oil tanker that was refueling us. Not wanting to get into a fight with a soaking wet tanker man, I recoiled the hose. Almost immediately, we went to abandon ship stations. I discovered I had forgotten to wear a belt so Ben fed one out through the window casing. After all, who wants to abandon ship without a belt?!? I arrived at lifeboat #1 and discovered that it would be impossible to lower the boats because again the tanker men would take a dim view of our abandoning ship right on top of their tanker. Also, it would be difficult to row while your lifeboat was perched on top of a tanker's deck. The drill was over almost before it started and was a farce! The reason the boats on the port side weren't lowered was that they would have landed right in the middle of a railroad terminal and that also might have been rather embarrassing!

The FCC inspection was also a farce. He looked at our licenses and at one log sheet and that was about it. He didn't even question the ham rig, which is semi-illegal. Phil took him to dinner on the ship and got buddy-buddy with him. He ended up offering us the use of his Sprite car whenever we are in Buffalo!

I washed my laundry this afternoon and saw some of Buffalo. It's one of the crummiest, dirtiest cities I've ever seen. There is trash laying everywhere and millions of drunken panhandlers walk about. One of the "AB's" (Able Bodied Seamen or deck hands) got knocked on the head and robbed of $180 last night.

Seven waitresses and some of the guys got back on tonight so the ship is coming to life again. Mike Calabash crawled out of his hole on the fantail roaring drunk tonight. He swore and started cutting up as usual and then grabbed Kay's pocketbook, Ben Hur, and threw it off the fantail. He really got would up and started quoting poetry and finally swore at all the officers he hated, called the ship an insane asylum and a three ring circus, and threw his work gloves overboard saying "I quit!" and then instructing them to bring the book back! Ralph was on the fantail and was necking with Lorrie. He had laid his hat down beside him. With a little coaxing, Mike turned his talents on attempting to throw the cap overboard. He made several attempts but he never quite could steal it, much to the delight of the spectators. He finally gave another burst of swearing and yelled "Good night!" and disappeared down his hole again. He is tanked up all the time and is quite funny.

July 6, 1210: During our tugging operations, five waitresses were snowed by the suave Englishmen aboard the Melanie Fair and ended up living aboard the tug for a couple of days! This obviously didn't look good and the end result was that they were all fired—permanently! Today, a new waitress from the South American got on at Cleveland. She's pretty ugly.

July 7, 0135: Last night the sun set on an absolutely crystal clear sky. We were in the Detroit and St. Clair Rivers so it was very beautiful out. I braved a very cold breeze to stand on "A" Deck foreward for an hour as we came into the Imperial Oil docks at Sarnia, Ontario at 2215. There are several refineries in the last several miles and it is quite a sight to see them all lit up and belching smoke and spewing flames into the night air. Tonight, just before my watch, Ben received an SOS but in his excitement, only copied a small portion of it. We both calmed down and it was sent again at 0023 and I copied the following:

"SOS SOS DE NOC 070312 GMT aircraft type Piper Comanche reported position 4250 W 3600 N e route Bermuda to Azores at 070035 GMT intends to ditch at 070335 GMT in position 39.05 N

35.00 W. Vessels in vicinity keep a sharp lookout and assist if possible."

I was very surprised when I heard several stations broadcasting on the distress frequency. We ceased operations immediately to keep the frequency clear. Hmmmm—creeping lidism!! We are now on our regular schedule and are heading to Parry Sound, Ontario.

July 8, 0208: We left Detroit over one hour late yesterday and so could not make Parry Sound. Instead, we sailed to Sault Saint Marie. We arrived at 1915. Tom and I went bowling and then saw some fireworks that had been postponed from the 4th because of rain. It was a very impressive display for the small town. After that, I met three kids, one named Bob Knick who knew Mike Johnson (a fraternity brother) and was from Anderson, IN, who drove me up to see the locks. They looked just like any other locks I'd ever seen. We sailed at 2300 for Mackinac Island and will arrive at 0800 today.

There is a couple aboard that is causing quite a stir around the ship. The male half is very suave with mustache, etc. and looks like a Hollywood producer. All the girls are snowed. The female half is very beautiful! She wears Leopard skin things on deck and very low cut gowns to the dining room. She smokes from a long cigarette holder and looks like the producer's actress wife (or?). Wherever they go, they put on quite a show and seem to like the commotion they cause. Regarding the girl—all the boys are snowed!!

I received a call on 500 KC Morse code saying that manned life rafts had been sighted. This might be from the ditched plane. I received it from NMF-Boston at 0120.

July 9, 0010: We spent the whole morning from 0808 to 1148 at Mackinac Island but when we docked, Ben (on watch from 8 to 12) lay down for a "short nap" as we only have to answer the phone in port. Ben's nap lasted all morning with the result that he didn't wake me up in time to get off at the Island. In fact, I had to wake him up to make the dinner announcements!!

We have a bunch of Episcopalian ministers aboard for some sort of a convention. They have been holding meetings all day for several days but tonight must be their last night for they really let go! Most of them got slightly polluted and Dave Graham (about 40 years old), leader of the ship's band, remarked in all seriousness to one of the kids in the band that any one of the ministers could drink any of the kids under the table.

Before going on watch at night, I have a few cups of coffee at the officer's mess in the galley. There are usually a strange conglomeration of engineers, patrolmen and the like down there also. Tonight they brought a silver book down there entitled

"Famous Nudes"! Because of my keen interest in high-class literature and the finer things in life, I decided to investigate. But, upon opening the book, I got knocked across the room by a tremendous shock! It turned out that the thing had a battery and an induction coil in it and the two covers were metal contacts!! We had a lot of fun playing the trick on each unsuspecting newcomer to the group!

We are organizing our new Crew Show, which we will present at the Grand Hotel on Mackinac Island on Labor Day. We will put on the production "Down in the Valley" providing that the rights don't cost too much. Joyce and Wayne will star and I was pleasantly surprised to know that the only other male major role was awarded to me! I hope we can do it because I've always wanted to do a singing-acting part like this.

We are bound for Chicago and should arrive at 1115 EST. There is a big full moon out and the sky is fairly clear. It is very beautiful playing its light on some islands off the Michigan shore and dancing on the choppy waters of Lake Michigan!

July 10, 0012: Weather is rainy. Today I almost pulled what is known as a "Claude Sheets". It seems that a radio operator by this name arrived in Chicago on board the North America last year and was met by two girl friends at the same time. There he was, waving from the radio shack and the two girls no more than 20 feet apart were returning the gesture each oblivious of the other. Needless to say, this caused much consternation.

Today, Karen Hausman came down to see the ship. I haven't seen her for a year and it was fun to hear her bubbling over with fun. She loves being a Theta (Phi Kappa Theta) and misses school. She was the only freshman selected as a fraternity favorite. Also, she is the only freshman female member of the school paper. Mom, Dad and Karen arrived at 12 and we went to the Chicago Athletic Club for lunch. Then we toured the ship. The whistles blew and as we were leaving, we met Jim Hallstrom on the dock. He had had some difficulty getting down so he didn't see the ship. He probably will be down next week. He wanted a picture of Karen and me so I put my arm around her and he took it. I looked up and there was Joyce on the poop deck looking very puzzled. I said goodbye and rushed to the poop deck whereupon Joyce and I put our arms around each other. I looked down and there was Karen looking very puzzled! Right now, I'm exhausted!! Everybody is back on and saying hello again and all. We're practicing for the Crew Show already and the old North is humming again just like she used to.

We changed the SSB rig to commercial frequencies today. WAY Chicago is just on the air and WMI Lorain will be on by Monday. We are the first ship on the Great Lakes to use this form of transmission. We are still running radio checks and putting it through its paces but I know from my experience as a ham that this method will one day be common place and AM will be unheard of. The improvement is quite noticeable!

July 11, 0012: Got into Mackinac today at 1430 and Joyce and I walked around to the left of the Island. I think next time, we will rent bicycles and try to go all the way around the Island.

Tonight we had a Crew Show meeting. The royalties for "Down in the Valley" will probably be too much so we will do a variety show. I'm going to be singing a solo every Sunday night from now on for the variety show.

The evening sunset was very beautiful. There was a hazy lake steam covering the lake and the sun shining through it made the whole sky pink. This also tinted the water pink.

July 12, 0012: We docked at Sarnia, Ontario on the St. Clair River to take on fuel and the passengers were cleared through customs and immigration to go ashore. This is not usually done. We left at 1145-about one hour late-but still made it to Detroit on time. While we were crossing Lake St. Clair, I received the following from a lady with a high-pitched excited voice on channel 51. "Calling anyone, calling anyone. Come in!" That was all. The Coast Guard stations in the area tried to make contact with the yacht but there were no further transmissions. They sent boats out to investigate but, as far as I know, found nothing.

Phil has been running around the ship trying to locate the source of some interference that is messing up our radios. He is throwing everyone into complete panic as he moves around the ship with a portable radio turning off the power to the beer coolers in the bar, the ice boxes, dishwashers, etc..trying to locate the source. We have finally located a motor that is causing much of the trouble and that will be rebuilt tonight.

A bunch of guys on the poop deck watched the sun set tonight. We listened to an FM station from Detroit that had an excellent jazz show on. Lake Erie is very calm and it is another beautiful night. The moon is almost full and is shining prettily down on the calm lake. There is a surprising amount of shipping going on on the Lakes and we can see as many as 10 ships at a time gliding along with their lights shining.

July 13, 0010: Today (June 12) we docked at Buffalo and I worked from 12 to 4. At 4, Joyce Mel, Andrea and I went to a barbeque at Paul Anderson's house (a friend of Mel's) in Cleveland Hills. They are very pleasant and Mr. Anderson kept us in stitches telling about pranks he pulled in college. For example, rolling a firecracker under the Dean of Men's bed one night! When we got back at 6:15, Dick Holmes was on the dock. Joyce and I showed him around the ship. It was real good to see him again. We made some real hasty plans for next Tuesday, which is Joyce's 21st birthday.

Last night on the fantail, there was quite a party! A big jar was filled with lemonade and a fifth of gin and sunk onto the fantail. Everyone sat around drinking from paper cups. Two more jars were brought with lemonade in one and cherry juice in the other and, of course, more gin. Soon everyone became jovial and a few overdid it. Annie, our maid, got drunk and sat in the corner making out with one of the patrolmen! She could hardly stand and finally staggered back to the harem!

Bob Bond and Tom Strable had a drinking contest at Dan's with Bob winning "somewhere after 14 beers when I lost count" when Tom got sick. Bob still is not feeling too good and since he is Night Messman, he's having a bad time on his job. Jackie, a waitress, broke up with her fiancé who joined the drinking party but he didn't do too well. He quietly slipped underneath the table and passed out after a "few" beers.

July 14, 0022: Yesterday, we arrived in Detroit with our usual welcome of fog and rain. It never fails!! This was our first rainy day for quite a while. We are now on Lake Huron proceeding to Parry Sound and there is a 25 MPH wind blowing straight down the Lake onto our bow. This coupled with the 10 to 15 MPH headway we are making makes it quite windy on deck. There are big waves on the Lake tonight and we are seesawing back and forth. I was up on the bow watching us hit the waves. We dive into them and the spray sails out 25 to 50 feet and comes up onto the Promenade Deck occasionally. It's very pretty. Tom, Kathy, Joyce and I played bridge on the fantail tonight. I'm playing quite a bit and am finally getting to know what it's all about and what to do.

0100: Just been listening to the Democratic convention. Kennedy got the nomination.

July 15, 0024 EST: Got up at 0930 after 4-1/2 hours sleep for a Crew Show rehearsal. Apparently no one else thought it important for less than half the kids showed up and it was cancelled. Tomorrow we have a Fire and Lifeboat Drill at Mackinac at 0900, which means I only get 4 hours again tonight for a total of 8 hours sleep for 64 hours! This isn't too good an idea! We finally made Parry Sound, Ontario today after a pleasant trip through Georgian Bay. Parry Sound is a quaint Northwoods town with rocky wooded hills and islands all over. I wish we had more time there. We had a Crew Show rehearsal and then a meeting at 2200 to plan the new show. I'm on the committee that puts people into the different numbers

1330: I'm about ready to quit!!! I just had a crazy man up in the shack that completely tore the place apart. I think he was out of his head. He wanted a call put through to a doctor in Chicago. I must have instructed him a million times on how to use the phone but he couldn't understand. He finally just stood there and screamed "hello, hello, hello!!" while pushing the push-to-talk switch on and off rapidly. He finally got the thing turned on and said the following: "They said 'All ashore who are going ashore' and so the Captain, the Radio Operator and I are the only ones left. It's very cold and even Mr. Webster, the big shot, is very inhospitable. They're all confused because they ran up on a sandbar." This is almost word for word as near as I could remember. He ranted and raved after the call was over about paying outlandish prices for the call. We were on for 18 minutes and WLC charged us for only 3 but he was still unhappy. As he left he opened the door but didn't hold on to it and it got caught in the breeze and smashed against the railing showering glass for 20 feet straight back. It's lucky no one was sunning there. Rosy, the Carpenter, just came and took it away for some new glass.

July 16, 0000: Yesterday was a hectic day! I found out more about this character who devastated the radio room. According to Ruth Smith, the Nurse, he is a chronic alcoholic. So I guess he was just a wee bit under the weather when he made the call.

We had a Fire and Lifeboat Drill as usual and lowered the boats and tore all around the harbor. We left Mackinac Island but no sooner did we get out in the harbor than trouble developed and we dropped an anchor. It turned out that one of the anchors had fouled when it was dropped in the Lifeboat Drill and we had dragged it out into the harbor with us. This obviously was not conducive to good piloting so the situation was remedied and we got under way again. At 1600 we had Crew Show practice for "Oklahoma", a number for Sunday night and then the Placement Committee met for a while. At 2100, we had the regular Crew Show.

July 17, 0050: We docked at Chicago at 1119 and I met Bob Martin. We walked down to a barbershop on Grand Avenue so that I could get a haircut. The barber must have been foreign because I talked with him for 15 minutes and the only thing I understood was "Kennedy" and "Democrat". I just kept saying, "yes" whenever I thought he was asking me a question. Unfortunately, I must have agreed to the wrong things for I got a horrible haircut and the screwball charged me $2.25 for the butchering. I had Port Watch (12-4) so I got back right away and Bob left to go lifeguarding at Wilmette. We rehearsed Oklahoma and I worked on my solo, "I Got Plenty O' Nuttin", which I will sing tonight. We played bridge on the fantail but Joyce and I didn't have very good cards.

July 18, 0015: Yesterday we arrived at Mackinac Island ½ hour early as usual. It was one of the first times we've hit the Island when it wasn't sunny and brilliant. The sun was out but there was quite a bit of Lake steam. We rehearsed our numbers for tonight's show until 1545 and then Joyce and I climbed up by the old Fort. Joyce told me that she loved me. (We had developed quite a romance. I didn't report much on our activities or relationship in the diary because the other Radio Operators were reading it and I didn't want too much to get around the ship. I told Joyce days earlier that I loved her but this was the first time she responded to me with those magic words)

I made my debut as a soloist tonight! Thank God I don't have to sing for a living!!! The moist air gave me a raspy tone. The first time through, I was off key in parts but the second time through, I relaxed and it sounded ok.

Mike, the AB, crawled out of his hole in the fantail again roaring drunk! He started to sing a song and everyone egged him on. He finished and sat down with the choice comment, "I've got to sit down and rest. I'm like the waitresses. I've got my brain in my ass!" This, of course, threw the whole place into pandemonium! The girls were embarrassed but most of the guys just about split. He struggled to his feet again and started to sing "St. James Infirmary". He inserted many funny statements in between lines such as (Song) "...saw my baby there. She was stretched out on a long white table..." (aside) "and that's the way I like 'em". He kept us in stitches and even tried a little dancing. Then, he put his arm around Kathy and wiggled his mustache and tried to make out. Finally, he got tired, swore at everyone, staggered to his hole and slipped down to the Flicker.

July 19, 0120: Yesterday, as we neared Detroit, we ran into the usual fog and thunderstorms! I think the city is jinxed! The radio shack was full of static electricity and the receivers were whining with corona discharge. I drew 1-1/2 inch sparks from the main antenna to ground!

Today is Joyce's 21st birthday so in Detroit yesterday, I dashed up town and bought her some yellow roses, her favorite, and a cultured pearl on a gold necklace.

Last night the committee that I'm on met and put the kids in the various numbers for the new Crew Show. It was a big job because the kids all work different hours. In order to get a common time for rehearsal, this has to be taken along with problems of voice, acting, etc.

0048: I copied a Code telegram from WBL Buffalo. It's always fun to work the Code rig because it's such a challenge. However, WBL sends as though he was using his left leg that had polio and now was in a cast because of an automobile accident! What I'm trying to say is that the jerk can't send good code!

July 20, 0010: Yesterday was Joyce's birthday and we went all out on a celebration. At 0600, when the Harem was unlocked, Mel set 25 yellow roses, Joyce's favorite flower, inside the Harem door. When the girls discovered this it caused quite a stir and helped shake up the troops and start the day off right. When Phil went down to breakfast, he delivered three fake radio telegrams including one signed by: "Mr. Lucking, Mr .Goebel, Mr. Dow, Capt. Picard and the crew of the North and South American". At noon, Mel, Andy, Joyce, Patti and I met Paul Anderson and we all went to Niagara Falls, NY. We ate lunch and then decided to take the tour in which you walk up to the foot of the American Falls. We entered and separated to two dressing rooms and they threw some long underwear at us mumbling something bout getting wet. We all laughed but decided to play their silly game! Next, we put on slippers made out of some burlap material and finally a big yellow heavy raincoat. We met the girls and took an elevator down from the upper river to the river level below the Falls. We then walked out on wooden stairways and platforms around the base of the falls. It's a good thing we wore our "blue pajamas" and raincoats because we got drenched! They must have a sense of humor though because at the place where the water is cascading down on you there is a sign saying "No Smoking"!! After Niagara, we bought a bottle of champagne and went to Paul's house for dinner. There was enough champagne for one drink each. It was Joyce's first and I guess she liked it.

Tonight on the poop deck and later the fantail, there was a big drinking party and about 10 of the crew got bombed out of their minds. Tom could hardly stand and Mike, the AB, got caught by Joe, the First Mate. I don't think he'll be with us too much longer.

July 21: We docked at Detroit again but this time the sun made a concentrated effort to peek out from the clouds and it didn't even rain a drop! I'm working on some new numbers for the Crew Show and after dinner last night, I picked up Mike's trumpet and blew a few notes in the deserted ballroom. I lost my lip in 5 minutes so it looks like I'll never be a trumpet player!! This Sunday, I think I'll sing "Some Enchanted Evening". The whole group for the new Crew Show rehearsed the new songs for 1-1/2 hours and we all got hoarse.

I spent most of my morning watch reading a book on bridge so I could find out why Joyce and I never won when we played! Ye Gods! The game's confusing!

As we left Detroit, a rather amusing incident occurred. Along side of the dock there are groups of 8 or 10 pilings measuring 10 to 15 feet long and 4 feet thick. The Captain backed our stern out into the river as usual and backed away from the dock. He then gave her full ahead but he swung the stern around too fast with the result that we charged back into the dock. All the natives and dockworkers scrambled for cover as we hit the dock. We caught one of the groups of pilings in a hatchway and ripped and bent them to an angle of about 45 degrees. As we steamed away from Detroit, the dock was a scene of pandemonium! The dockworkers were jumping up and down and shaking their fists while the tourists guffawed! Capt. Picard blushed as he left the flying bridge but had a stiff upper lip and an expression of confidence that seemed to say, "Better luck next time." We've been thinking of buying decals to paste on the side of the radio shack. We could chalk up a dock, a sandbar, some running lights and a couple of seagulls!

July 22, 0030: At 10:05 PM EST yesterday, Ben copied the following: "Severe weather forecast: Lake Superior, Northern Lake Michigan and Northern Lake Huron. Severe weather forecast 9:50 PM EST Thursday. A few severe thunderstorms with hail and local winds in excess of 65 knots are expected over Lake Superior spreading southeastward into Northern portions of Lakes Michigan and Huron tonight from the present time until 3 AM EST Friday. There is a possibility of an isolated tornado shore area or waterspout over the Lake." It's fairly rough out now. The trough is southwest and we are going northwest so we are in a quartering sea. It seems to be quieting down now. However it's <u>nothing</u> like the Holland deadhead. The radio crew on the South are a bunch of lids! I've been calling Tony, the operator on my watch on 500KC at 0200 each morning on a pre-arranged schedule but I have yet to hear him answer! I just got through talking to him on SSB and he hadn't even heard the severe weather forecast! (Again, the Radio Operators were very important. The Captain and Mates relied on us to provide weather information, etc. to them). Tonight, we will pass the South and if I can't raise him on Morse Code, I'll quit.

We rehearsed the new Crew Show last night and then played bridge for an hour. Mike, the AB, is still with us in spite of his spree. I worked through Parry Sound yesterday and didn't even get ashore.

July 23, 0056: Mackinac Island yesterday. It was sunny as usual! Our Fire and Lifeboat Drill was fast as we didn't abandon ship. My fire station is just above the Sun Deck where the 2nd Mate walks "counting heads." I have a peculiar urge to turn the hose on him and wash him overboard. He's pretty grouchy. I must control myself, however!

It was a bit chilly coming down Lake Michigan this afternoon. On days like this, the Poop Deck is really funny looking. Most of the kids come up in bathing suits hoping for the sun to peek out so they can tan but everyone gets cold and rolls up in blankets. It is amusing to see everyone lying all over the Poop Deck in blankets!

Captain's Dinner was tonight as usual and I had a thick slice of prime rib-rare! This is by far their best meal and is the best meat I've ever had! (All the food on board was excellent and was "all you can eat". I put on quite a few pounds over the summer. We ate at the officer's table on a little platform and wore our uniforms. The Captains and Mates sat at one table and the Radio Operators and other officers at another).

Tonight, we put on the regular Crew Show or as Ben says, "Crude Show"! After that, we played an hour worth of bridge. Reading that book must have paid off because I made a Grand Slam!!

July 24, 0120: Yesterday Mom and Dad got on for a run to Mackinac for a convention. Grandma came down to see them off. She's still a live wire at 82 and we're trying to get her to take a cruise. She'd have a ball! We were one-hour late leaving Chicago due to river traffic. I arranged with Mr. Beauregard to sit at Joyce's table with the folks on first sitting. This way they'll be able to see the approach to Mackinac. Joyce and I played Mom and Dad in bridge and we beat them. We held real good cards as usual. We saw and did everything tonight including a short visit with Mike who was his usual drunk self. He got into a fistfight with McGee tonight and would have thrown him overboard "except for the wire, retaining fence that stopped me!"

July 25, 0148: Ate lunch with my parents again. It was sunny coming into Mackinac as usual and they had a real good time watching our approach. Joyce and I went to their room in the Grand Hotel and we all sat around and talked and watched the beautiful view. I sang "I Got Plenty of Nuttin'" again tonight and it went over pretty good. I'm still not much of a singer but I'm improving!

As we docked at Mackinac, I looked on the bridge and saw, to my surprise, that Joe Testian, the 1st Mate, was docking us. He also took her out and the rumor is that he will be the new Captain as of Detroit.

July 26, 0011: I slept through our stop at Sarnia as usual. To our surprise, it was a beautiful sunny day even when we hit Detroit, so Joyce and I sunbathed. Joe docked us again and the Captain in civilian clothes walked slowly away from her with only one quick, sad look back. It was a sad scene. The rumor is that he will have four days of medical checks and will, in all probability, return at that time. However, there has been no official announcement of any kind.

July 27: Docked at Buffalo with the sun shinning, temperature in the high 80's and very humid. When I got off work, Joyce and I went to Dan's.

Last night I saw quite a storm! The wind was hard from the south yet the storm came from the northwest. I stood on "A" Deck forward and watched it. Lightning was hitting about once every two or three seconds. I went back to the shack and sparks were really flying!! We had to ground the cases of all the equipment together. I decided that this was not the safest spot on the ship and so I evacuated rather hastily. All of a sudden, it was upon us. Lightning hit all around us and it rained like crazy! The wind had shifted onto our bow (West) and the rain flew back all the way to the first set of stairs on "B" Deck. Looking forward, all I could see was a wall of rain and the bow was obscured. We blew three blasts on the whistle about every 15 seconds. This means, "I can't see a darn thing!" The decks became a stream of flowing water. It passed us soon and we didn't get the main part of the storm. Surprisingly, the Lake didn't get rough and we hardly rolled at all. We are pitching and rolling a bit now and it is still raining a bit but I don't think it's enough to bother anyone. The wind has swung to the north now.

Mike made himself a cowboy lasso and tried to "Corral himself a gal" but without too much success. He said he could never be a cowboy though because he was riding a horse once and told it to go hard starboard but the horse became confused at this and threw him. He finally got mad as usual and cussed everyone out and then crawled back down his hole!

July 28, 0012: A beautiful sunny day until we got near Detroit! A big dark cloud hung over Detroit and lifted just a few minutes before we left. Joe docked us at Detroit without a bump. He has never docked her until now but he is doing a much better job than Capt. Picard! At Detroit, they have completely replaced the pilings Picard broke off. They are bright and new and are rather conspicuous! Tonight, the new Crew Show committee met and then we watched the lights at Sarnia—always a pretty sight.

July 29, 0106: We left Detroit about one hour late so our schedule was again changed from Parry Sound to Sault Saint Marie. We've had beautiful weather and Lake Huron was absolutely calm this morning except for a few wind ripples. The St. Mary's River is extremely beautiful and the air is saturated with a pine scent that intoxicates me! Yesterday evening and this morning, there is a fabulous display of Northern Lights! Half the nights, there is usually some display but tonight is rare. Half the sky is covered and fingers of light stretch to the treetops and in great arcs overhead. The night is clear and the stars are shinning through brilliantly. It's good to be alive!! (My watch was 12-4 in the afternoons and early morning hours. With little to do in the night, I was able to really enjoy the night sky and all of its wonders).

July 30, 0035: We are proceeding down Lake Michigan with a strong wind blowing us in the face. It's a little bit rough and I think we'll cut across right away to hit Wisconsin to get out of the waves. We stopped at Mackinac Island and it was sunny and warm. Fire and Lifeboat Drill as usual except someone stole our drill winch so we had to crank it up by hand! Mom and Dad were there and got some pictures. We sat around and talked most of the time and then they watched the Crew Show. We spent most of the evening on the bow watching several squall lines.

2310: Mom and Dad got off in Chicago today and so did Phil and Ben. Two men, Mr. Gause and Mr. Schroeder, came aboard for one week. They used to operate the radios about 30 years ago and they come back every year for a one-week cruise. They weren't on for more than five minutes before we all sat around having a drink from a bottle produced from a suitcase full. Next on the agenda was a call to Mr. Colley to renew their charge account for liquor. Their suitcase contained an estimated "two hours worth". These guys should be a lot of fun in the coming weeks. I'll be working 8 to 12 while they're aboard.

As we left Chicago we ran into some big waves for about 3 or 4 hours. A strong (25 MPH) NW wind had been blowing since 0230 last night and it piled up some good waves. Ralph and Mr. Beauregard immediately got sick and only three out of the six at our table made dinner. I gulped down a big steak dinner with no trouble at all. I'm not going to take pills anymore (I've only taken two) and see how it works. If tonight was any indication, I'm OK. All the waitresses took Dramamine but still some of them got sick. Most of the passengers didn't make it through their cocktails even!! Most of them slipped quietly away or made mad dashes for the strategically place paper bags. It has calmed down quite a bit now and there is just a small amount of pitching.

July 31, 2215: I ate breakfast in the dining room fo the first time today and it was very good and filling as all their other meals. The 8 to 12 watch is very good. The morning zipped by and I lay out in the sun all afternoon. I got the first sun tan I've had since the first Seaway cruise and it feels real good. We arrived at Mackinac at 1500 and Joyce and I rented bicycles and rode all the way around the Island. It's a very beautiful trip. We were almost around when we took a road inland. We climbed up a high hill and tried to locate one of the many caves on the Island without success. Then we raced back down the hill. I went first and took off like a streak of lightning. I gathered speed and was flying along when I came to the last curve and realized that I was traveling too fast. I hit the brakes and skidded on the loose gravel. Next I calmly mowed down several bushes and frightened a couple of frogs but lo and behold, I had discovered a new passage to the foot of the cliff!! In honor of this history-making event, the trail was claimed in the name of the North American and named Bay's boo boo drive.

Tonight was Variety Show and I sang my solo. I now have lots of confidence but it still sounds just as bad. I find that if I go out and smile and look as though I know how to sing, that this helps the audience to grin and bear it.

August 1, 2204: Today was very busy. This 8 to 12 watch is good because I finally have some work to do!! I used over half a log sheet this morning alone.

We almost had an accident occur off our stern as we entered the St. Clair River. A small freighter called Security (Security is a form of radio call designed to alert ships in the area to a boat's intentions.) twice saying it was backing out of one of the coal docks. A big 400-500 foot tanker, the SS Druckenmiller, was coming towards this dock but apparently was unaware what was going on. The freighter pulled out and saw the ship bearing down on it but tried to pull out in front of it anyway and pass on one whistle. (This means that he intended to pass port side to port side. A diagram is at this point in the diary). The tanker said "You can't make it on one whistle!" but the freighter kept saying "One whistle! One whistle!" The tanker went full reverse and just missed cutting the freighter in two! Then they both went on the air and yelled at each other. The tanker swore repeatedly, highly illegal, and reported the incident to the Coast Guard. They yelled at each other some more and then they got so excited that they both were transmitting at the same time. One said, "I don't even want to talk to you anymore!" and that was that!!

I lay in the sun again all afternoon. I'm getting a good tan for a change. It was even sunny in Detroit today.

August 2, 2222: Arrived in Buffalo today with the weather humid and windy and spent until 1500 with Federal Fire and Lifeboat Drill. The wind was blowing strong in my face and I got drenched from head to foot when I turned my fire hose on.

I saw "Hercules" downtown and it was stupid! The Lake is fairly calm tonight and there is a refreshing cool breeze blowing!

August 3: Rained in Detroit as usual today but cleared later in the afternoon after we left, as usual. Before I went down to dinner, John Gause asked if I had had my vitamins. I was puzzled but wasn't when he nodded to a half full bottle of Whisky!! I hadn't had vitamins for a long time and knew Mom would be pleased to know I was taking them again! I had a very enjoyable supper. The two men are not as wild as all the stories I heard indicated. They just work and then lock themselves up and drink. How dull!

We stopped at Sarnia for fuel tonight and will do so for the rest of the season.

August 4: Made the run to Sault Saint Marie, Ontario with good weather. This is really a beautiful run. The moon is shining brightly and dancing on the water. The trees in the background make quite a sight. We docked on the Canadian side for the first time this season. We will dock here once more and then dock on the American side for the rest of the season.

August 5: The cook goofed because there was a sudden outbreak of dysentery. The Radio Department was temporarily out of commission and the watch was changed about once every 5 minutes! Ugh!!

August 7, 0012: I'm back on my 12 to 4 watch because Ben and Phil are back. As a result, I worked all morning and afternoon again. There wasn't much of a breeze and the fumes from the smokestacks gave me a bad headache that I still have. The moon is out now and is full. It is as bright as day out and very pretty.

August 8, 0015: We have had some very strange weather! As we came up Lake Michigan, I received a report of waterspout danger for the central Lake Michigan area. We were North of the area so it didn't bother us but we are getting the tail end on Lake Huron tonight, as the winds are westerly. Right now the winds are 40-45 MPH and the barometer is 29.08—very low. I can actually feel the difference in pressure and it is much the same sensation as flying in an airplane. We are hugging the west shore so we are in the lee but shortly we will be abreast of Saginaw Bay and there we will have no protection. Even now at Thunder Bay, it is rough and we are rolling quite a bit.

In Mackinac today, the weather was also strange! As we docked, it was very cloudy and looked like rain so I took my raincoat. By the time we tied up and I got out on the dock, it was almost completely clear and I almost returned my raincoat. Joyce and I decided to see Fort Mackinac and we were halfway up the steps when it clouded over and we suddenly got caught in a deluge. The weather was changing every 5-10 minutes.

I sang my solo again last night and it went pretty good. I think singing is fun and I especially enjoy the nice comments people make. A man last week, for instance, came backstage after the show with a tear in his eye. He grabbed my arm and with a look of pity said, "Courage, son!" I'm not quite sure how to take this, however!! (This was an attempt at a joke. In reality, this didn't happen!)

August 9, 0145: We docked at Detroit today and as usual, we were greeted with a 15-minute deluge! In the process of a futile attempt to find a Notary to get my Amateur Radio license renewed, Joyce and I came across a crazy "Coney Island" hot dog joint. The dogs were good and were completely smeared with relishes and other goo! We worked on songs for the new Crew Show tonight. Wednesday, a professional will come aboard to help us with the choreography.

August 10, 0105: Buffalo today and Joyce and I saw Alfred Hitchcock's new movie, "Psyco". It was real good and exciting as he is famous for. We had a real exciting evening. About 2230, while I was on the fantail, the engine slowed down. I sensed something wrong and as I peered over the side, I saw the safety valve blow and then our emergency generator on the radio shack started. I ran up to investigate and discovered we had run across a disabled motorboat. It was a 23-foot JAFCO Seamaster #9M280. The weather was very rough and the boat was bobbing like a cork. It had an anchor out so it could head into the waves and if it wasn't for this, I think it would have capsized. The pilothouse was in a complete panic because when they turned on their big radar, they blew a fuse leaving them completely in the dark without power or steering control. The situation was remedied and they got spotlights on the boat. We called the Coast Guard stations on Lake Erie on channel 51 phone for ten minutes without an answer but finally raised NMD-Cleveland on code. In the mean time, the pilothouse had contacted two other ships, the Jos. S. Scobelle and the T. J. McCarthy, who changed course to relive us. We are on a very tight schedule and didn't want to waste too much time. Most of this time, we were trying to get our position across to Cleveland but they apparently panicked in all the fuss. We left and about 0034, the Scobelle radioed it had picked up the three men aboard and was towing their boat to Erie. Meanwhile, Erie Coast Guard came to life and decided to play hero and send out a Coast Guard cutter. The guy at the base station started calling the 40-footer with a voice that sounded as though he was handling emergency traffic for the Titanic! The funny thing is, he couldn't contact the Coast Guard boat and so the thing will probably circle the area for hours while the boat and men are safe on their way to Erie! Hooray for the Coast Guard...To the Rescue!! (I have other vivid memories of this encounter that were not recorded in the diary. After checking in at the Radio Shack, I worked my way along a narrow catwalk back to the stern to man a searchlight. The ship lurched and I was launched halfway overboard and just barely held on. Also, the men in the motorboat were laying on the seats with their arms and legs wrapped around the seats holding on for dear life...quite a sight. My write-up leaves the impression that we just left them but in fact, we maneuvered up wind of them to calm the seas they were facing and didn't leave until the other ship was on station.)

We blew the safety valve to shut down the engine for slow speed work. All this has put an additional burden on us because when we lost our power, we lost our gyroscope. It is oscillating back and forth now and should be back to normal in about nine hours. Meanwhile, we have to steer by magnetic compass—quite a job. Usually, it would take two days to calm down but Joe grabbed it by hand for several minutes and was able to tame it somewhat. This summer has really been a circus!!

0144: The Coast Guard cutter just stumbled across the Scobelle and was shocked to learn that the excitement was over. It is now sulking back home while the Scobelle tows the boat in!

August 11, 0030: Today was very cloudy again as we entered Detroit. However, we left just before the rain started this time! We were coming up to Lake St. Clair when we received a Mayday from a small boat. It didn't identify, give its location or assistance required but just kept yelling, "Emergency Call!" It turned out that they were five minutes from the Windsor Yacht Club and required oxygen. This was the second time I've heard a yacht in distress and both times they have failed to give any information about their trouble in their calls. Today this caused them 5-10 minutes delay and could have caused someone their life. Three Coast Guards and several ships all tried to make contact but the operator got panicky I guess.

0400: Just before I went off watch, I leaned back and closed my eyes and rested for a few minutes. The next thing I knew, I opened my eyes and there was Phil towering over me and it was three minutes later! Guess I was sleepy!!

August 12, 0024: It was very windy today as we traveled the St. Mary's River to Sault Saint Marie. We had just fixed the ventilator on top of our room so that it would draw more air into the room and it was merrily spinning and banging away. Suddenly, it stopped and I went to investigate. The darn thing worked so well and created such a vacuum that it grabbed the tail of one of my shirts and then sucked the whole shirt up into its mouth and ate it!! Emergency rescue operations were started immediately and I was able to fight the beast with my bare hands and unwind my slightly greasy shirt from its grip!!

Mary Pacard, the professional choreographer, is aboard and the whole crew has been rehearsing like crazy for the new Crew Show. Tonight, we worked 1-1/2 hours all through the port time. We were two hours late leaving the Soo because a ship lost its engine in the middle of the channel about 2:30 and was still in the process of being towed away!

August 13, 0020: A beautiful, sunny day at Mackinac again and it was especially nice because we didn't even lower the boats for Fire and Lifeboat Drill. The other number I'm in for the new Crew Show rehearsed today but we must all have left feet because they decided to delete the number! I was very surprised when Mrs. Packard called me by name and took me aside. She said I had talent and wanted me in some of the other numbers. I was so stunned that I volunteered and now I'm in "Standing on the Corner", which means more time shot for rehearsals. Ugh!

August 14: Gale warnings were up for central Lake area but it calmed down by the time we arrived. The new 100-foot aluminum balloon satellite is making passes about every two hours over us but the weather has been cloudy so no one has seen it yet. Also there should be meteor shower activity.

August 15: Beautiful weather in Mackinac yesterday. Our band was fired for playing poker until 4 AM and then sleeping through Cleveland. As a consequence, the Crew Show was a little thin yesterday but I managed to torture everyone with my solo as usual.

The wind has been blowing from the NE for a while now and Lake Huron is a little rough. We have a following, quartering sea so we are rolling. We haven't done this for quite a while and it feels good. I'm at the point where I get bored stiff when it's calm. I wish we'd get a good blow and run through some weather like we had on the Chicago-Holland deadhead!

August 16, 0123: Sunny for a change at Detroit today! A passenger brought up a Heathkit Mohican (ham radio) today for us to play around with for a while. It's a beauty! It weighs only a few pounds, covers up to 32 MC, completely transistorized, etc. All for only $100. We've been having a ball carrying it around listening to ham frequencies and commercial frequencies.

I got my previous day's wish about the weather because the roll steadily built up after I went to bed and at 0555, I found myself dangling from the bed during a roll. It was a good roll outside but it calmed down as we entered the bottom of Lake Huron. This is just as well because we probably would have lost the passengers. I braced myself better in the bunk and went back to sleep!

0330: The 100-foot satellite just passed over and I saw the darned thing. I get an overwhelming feeling of awe when I see it slowly moving through the sky. It's very impressive. Also, I saw some meteors—another fascinating phenomena.

August 17, 0033: We rehearsed the new Crew Show most of the afternoon and then Joyce and I saw a movie. We put on our new Crew Show for the first time tonight and it went real well.

I saw the satellite again at 2045. Tonight, we have the most brilliant display of Aurora I've ever seen! The radios are so dead that we can't talk to Lorain, Ohio from off of Erie—a path that is almost line-of-sight. It covers the whole Northern sky and Great big "waves" sweep rapidly upward.

0305: I saw the satellite pass over twice more tonight—at 0045 and at 0255.

August 28, 0240: We passed the Alexander T. Wood, a freighter involved in a collision that ran aground, at Amherstburg in the Detroit River today. They were unloading its cargo in an attempt to re-float it. The river was closed for three hours today starting at 1600 to try and pull it out.

Fred Gross, announcer for the Crew Show, got hit on the cheekbone with a flying shoe from a dance number last night and left the ship today with a fractured cheekbone. Mrs. Pacard, the dance instructor, also left.

I got some bad news today! The laundry in Buffalo stole my pants!! They couldn't get them done in time so I'm presently pantless!!!

Last night, the safety valve popped and we slowed down to almost a standstill and I couldn't figure out what had happened. Tonight, I found out that the Engine Department goofed and built too much steam up and it blew! This was very embarrassing to those involved and Cross was pretty honked off!

August 19, 0130: Very dull day. We went to Sault Saint Marie, Michigan and now we're going down the St. Mary's River.

August 20, 0009: Abandoned ship again this morning at Mackinac during Fire and Lifeboat Drill. This afternoon, I discovered the SSB rig was dead so we wouldn't be able to keep our schedule with WAY this morning. However, a well-placed blow on the operating table 2-1/2 feet from the left wall and 5-3/32 inches from the edge brought it swiftly back into operation. (Another feeble attempt at humor...measuring where I whacked the table). Crew Show tonight. Joyce sang her solo but forgot her words half way through. She stumbled on but was very shook when she came back stage.

August 21: It has rained most all day today. Mom and Dad came down with my car and Pixie (our dog) and it was good to see everyone and everything. I talked them into letting me get some two-meter FM gear for my car. I told Mr. Breight I would quit after the Labor Day cruise.

August 22: It was a beautiful day at Mackinac. I sang my solo again and got my first genuine and spontaneous compliment. I'm <u>sure</u> it won't go to my head though! I also met the Aunt of Dick Spencer, one of the wheels at Purdue. I recorded the show on my tape recorder and afterwards we played bridge on the fantail.

August 23, 0002: Beautiful day until we got near Detroit. A big black cloud chased us as usual and tried its best to drench us but didn't quite make it. Yesterday afternoon coming into Detroit, I decided it was too dull so I announced that calls to Detroit were 35 cents. I was swamped. I put through ten calls and was busy most of the afternoon. Tonight, I played bridge with Joyce, Tom and Phil. Our luck ran out. Since we began playing bridge, this was the first night that Joyce and I didn't have consistently good cards. We didn't have a hand all evening and got set four and five tricks consistently on hands that should have been good. To top it off, Phil and Tom made a Grand Slam in no trump. This is the best you can do! I'm disgusted!

August 24, 0015: They say tragedy strikes in threes and I guess it has. Oscar Hammerstein, of Rodgers and Hammerstein, died yesterday. These two men have been perhaps the greatest song writing team in history. The day before yesterday, Mr. Lucking, President of the Georgian Bay Lines, died. Things are in turmoil now and it will be next year probably before everything gets straightened out. Number 3—one of the colored Messmen missed the ship in Chicago. No one thought too much about this because it happens all the time. This time was different because two days later, he was in the morgue. No one knows anything else about it.

Joyce and I got our cards going in bridge again last night winning most of the hands and making a small slam. Right now, I'm doing battle with the bugs that chase us on Lake Erie.

August 25, 0110: Fred Gross got back on in Detroit yesterday and his face looks pretty good after his accident. The radio conditions have been very good and I heard PJC-Caribbean the other day. We docked at Sarnia tonight to refuel and Ben was on watch. He took off for five minutes to go to the head and get a candy bar. When he got back, the Captain was fuming because someone needed to be paged. The Captain fired him and told him to get off at Sault Saint Marie. I hope he changes his mind but that's the way it stands right now. I'm disgusted with this company. It is very poorly run and this is just another indication. They fire people without the least provocation!

August 26: Went to Sault Saint Marie and went shopping but escaped buying anything. This was a far cry from Buffalo where I bought a new suit and two pairs of shoes the last time we were there. It got pretty cold last night.

August 27: Put on our new Crew Show last night and Capt. Picard and his wife came down to see it! (Apparently, the Captain wasn't fired after all). This set a new precedent!

We ran into fog coming downbound on Lake Michigan in the afternoon but it lifted after a while and it is now a perfectly crystal clear night!

August 28: Docked at Chicago on a very muggy day. We were 1-1/2 hours late leaving Chicago because two of our four bearings had burned out and had to be replaced. They had been spraying water on them to cool them off for several hours. They were probably damaged at Ogdensburg.

Since the Outer Drive Bridge is closed to river traffic between 5 and 7, we had to get special clearance to get through at 5:30 PM. I'll bet many a late motorist cussed us out.

Mr. and Mrs. Helgren (friends of my parents) came aboard at Chicago and will sail to Detroit. They sailed on the North over 20 years ago.

John Flynn is now on the South American on Ben"s watch. (Apparently Ben didn't get fired after all!)

August 29: It was a foggy day today and the people didn't get to see Mackinac Island too well. We left there one hour late at 6:30 PM.

We did the Tuesday night Crew Show tonight. I guess they got too many complaints about my singing. (Another feeble attempt at humor).

August 30, 0010: The season is rapidly drawing to a close. Detroit welcomed us on our next to the last stop there with a big blow and lightning storm. The ship listed several degrees because of the wind and visibility was cut to a few hundred yards. We left Detroit at 5:30 PM so we are back on schedule again. The Helgren's got off today. It's too bad the weather wasn't nicer for them.

August 31, 0315: Today was our last day in Buffalo. We had a Federal Fire and Lifeboat Drill and it went OK. The Crew Show tonight was a panic. Most of the crew were so drunk they could hardly stand. I sang my solo for the last time and a passenger made an honest-to-goodness compliment. Wow! We had a songfest on the fantail afterwards.

September 1: Yesterday was unbearably hot. There was no wind relative to the ship and we all sweltered. As we broke out on Lake Huron, the wind freshened and a big lightning storm was visible off our port bow. I think we'll miss the center of it as it is proceeding eastward. This must be one of the most brilliant displays of Aurora of the summer tonight. The sky is cloudy but it is "back-lighted" all the way into the southern sky! The radios are in poor shape.

0046: We are in the lightning storm now and the radios are buzzing!

September 2: The rain and cloudy weather we've had since Chicago lifted yesterday in northern Lake Huron. Our trip to Sault Saint Marie, MI was very beautiful as it always is. The pine scent is something I will never forget. It is crystal clear out and cool jacket weather. A big storm hit the Frankfort area and knocked out telephone lines. Some of the crew tried phone calls to people they knew in the area but couldn't get through.

September 3: We put on our new Crew Show tonight for the last time before Mackinac Island. It had a very spastic beginning, however. The band started playing the overture and Tom Philbean, thinking this was the start of the opener, calmly walked out in front of the audience. I was second in line and followed him out. We realized our predicament as a sudden burst of laughter came from the audience. We calmly bowed to each other, tipped our hats to the audience and ran back stage.

Something very strange happened this morning. I saw a flying saucer!! It was round with a dome on top and had flashes of something coming out the sides. It looked like a searchlight playing on the clouds except that it was very erratic swooping up and down and out of sight. I called the pilothouse but Mark hadn't seen it. I looked some more and saw it swooping across the Lake towards our stern. I called Mark and he saw it too. We sat spellbound for about 30 seconds and then all of a sudden, we saw what it really was! There was a very bright moon out and the thing we saw was actually a seagull swooping around. The moonlight had made it appear the way we saw it. We both had a good laugh. It was scary for a while though and I found myself shaking! On the first pass, I would have sworn I had seen a real "saucer" but perhaps this is what they have been all along.

September 4: We ended our regular season yesterday at Chicago. We left at 1430 for Charlevoix, MI on a Labor Day Cruise. Jack Van Nest got off and Joan Torvick is real sad. Today, we'll put on our Crew Show at Mackinac Island. Joyce has a pretty bad cold and I hope she's better by show time.

(The last two pages of the diary are partially damaged so from here on is partial text and/or I have filled in the blanks as best I can)

Our radar was on the fritz and Julius ? came aboard to fix it. He worked on it for quite a while and when he finished, he discovered that he was out in Lake Michigan! Looks like he'll be making the trip to Charlevoix with us!! From there, he will board the South for their Seaway cruise.

September 5: We docked at Charlevoix again yesterday. They are still the same warm friendly people like before. This time they had a barbershop quartet sing in the Salon.

Then we went to Mackinac Island to put on our new Crew Show before a full house. It went good and I tape-recorded it. Afterwards I said goodbye to Joyce. This is our last??? Tomorrow morning???sign off at Chicago. The Island was beautiful as we left with all its sparkling light. We have a full moon to port and a good display of Aurora to starboard. The Mackinac Bridge is gorgeous at night. We are going over to Green Bay and then through the Sturgeon Bay Ship Canal and down Lake Michigan.

www.ingramcontent.com/pod-product-compliance
Lightning Source LLC
Chambersburg PA
CBHW031325040426
42443CB00005B/221
* 9 7 8 0 9 9 6 1 8 9 8 4 2 *